10 WONDERS

OF THE

ROSARY

Donald H. Calloway, MIC

Available from:
Marian Helpers Center
Stockbridge, MA 01263

Prayerline: 1-800-804-3823
Orderline: 1-800-462-7426
Websites: fathercalloway.com
marian.org

Library of Congress Catalog Number: 2018958118
ISBN 978-1-59614-486-6

Publication date: January 1, 2019
Solemnity of Mary, Mother of God

Imprimi Potest:
Very Rev. Kazimierz Chwalek, MIC
Provincial Superior
The Blessed Virgin Mary, Mother of Mercy Province
October 7, 2018
Feast of Our Lady of the Rosary

Nihil Obstat:
Dr. Robert A. Stackpole, STD
Censor Deputatus
October 7, 2018

Cover Image: "The Battle of Lepanto, with Don Juan of Austria Receiving
a Rosary from the Angel of Victory." (c.1883-1887). Ludwig Seitz (1844-
1908). Commissioned by Pope Leo XIII. Gallery of the Candelabra.
Vatican Museum. Vatican City. Used with permission.

[The Latin phrase in the painting is taken from the papal brief of Pope
Leo XIII, *Salutaris ille Spiritus precum* (December 24, 1883). It states:
"The rosary was instituted principally to implore the protection of the
Mother of God against the enemies of the Catholic name."]

Acknowledgments: Marian Fathers of the Immaculate Conception,
Mr. and Mrs. Donald & LaChita Calloway, Matthew T. Calloway,
Ileana E. Salazar, Teresa de Jesus Macias, Milanka Lachman,
Theresa Vonderschmitt.

MARIAN PRESS
STOCKBRIDGE   MA 01263

The rose is the queen of flowers, and so the rosary is the rose of all devotions and it is therefore the most important one.

It would hardly be possible for me to put into words how much Our Lady thinks of the holy rosary and of how she vastly prefers it to all other devotions.

St. Louis de Montfort

DEDICATION

To my mom,
LaChita G. Calloway.
You are a wonder of the rosary,
and I love you.

Acclaim for
10 Wonders of the Rosary

Father Calloway has done it again! His new book presents fascinating true stories — and exceptional wisdom from the saints — on the power of the rosary. This book is a must-read!

> **— Most Rev. Andrij Rabij, DD, JCL**
> Auxiliary Bishop of the Ukranian Catholic
> Archeparchy of Philadelphia

In captivating fashion, Fr. Calloway reminds us that the rosary is a divine gift that continues to work miracles. What is remarkable about the 10 wonders is that they are absolutely true!

> **— Very Rev. Benedict D. O'Cinnsealaigh, STD**
> President-Rector, Mount St. Mary's Seminary of the West
> Cincinnati, Ohio

This jewel of a book dazzles with historical accounts, spiritual insights, and personal testimony. Enrich your life and the lives of others — pray the rosary!

> **— Fr. George E. Schultze, SJ, PhD**
> President-Rector, St. Patrick's Seminary and University
> Menlo Park, California

10 Wonders of the Rosary is an inspirational refresher for the prayer warrior and an easy introduction to the rosary for the newcomer. You will "wonder anew" as you journey through this book.

— **Fr. Malachi Van Tassell, TOR, PhD**
President, Saint Francis University
Loretto, Pennsylvania

This book is the 11th wonder of the rosary! Read for yourself how Our Lady supports and sustains those who are devoted to her through the rosary. The rosary is our spiritual weapon!

— **Mother Marie Andre Campbell, PCPA**
Abbess of Our Lady of Solitude Monastery
Tonopah, Arizona

A thoroughly enjoyable and spiritually uplifting read. Once again, Fr. Calloway has made an excellent scholarly contribution to our understanding of the rosary. Even the devoted scholar of the rosary will find something new and fascinating!

— **Fr. Michael Mary Dosch, OP**
Novice Master of the Dominican Province of St. Joseph

Heartfelt devotion, solid Catholic doctrine, challenging moral exhortation, and compelling historical facts are a few of the many reasons why you should read *10 Wonders of the Rosary*. The rosary is the great spiritual weapon in the battle between the forces of Christ and the powers of hell!

— **Fr. William P. Casey, CPM**
Fathers of Mercy

In a compelling yet extraordinary manner, Fr. Calloway presents the power and wonder of the rosary for people of all ages. The rosary is the solution to the prevailing spiritual crises of our times. Read this book and be blessed!

— **Dick and Terry Boldin**
Founders, Rosary Evangelization Apostolate
Producers, *Power in My Hands* (Rosary Film)

10 Wonders of the Rosary delivers a shattering blow to the evil one. Every chapter left me in awe. An absolute must for every soldier of Jesus and Mary!

— **Thomas K. Sullivan**
Designer, "The Warrior's Rosary"

Contents

FOREWORD

INTRODUCTION

WONDER 1

The Rosary is of Divine Origin 11

WONDER 2

The Rosary is a Spiritual Weapon 23

WONDER 3

WONDER 4

WONDER 5

WONDER 6

WONDER 7

WONDER 8

WONDER 9

FOREWORD

The Church and the world are in great need of the wonders of the rosary.

After the miraculous victory of the Christian army over the powerful Muslim army at Lepanto in 1571, the Venetian senators proclaimed: "Neither valor, nor arms, nor armies, but Our Lady of the Rosary gave us victory!"

In modern times, the Blessed Virgin Mary herself in her various apparitions, especially in Lourdes and in Fatima, teaches us that the rosary is the most efficient, pleasing, and powerful prayer that she wants us to use against the evils of our time. Indeed, the rosary is the most apt means for people of every age and profession to be victorious in all spiritual battles.

As many saints and popes have related, no heart can remain cold or indifferent when meditating on the saving mysteries of Jesus Christ. Praying the holy rosary calms the anxious mind, comforts the burdened heart, and gives peace to the restless soul. Meditating on the mysteries of the rosary, Christians are given heavenly aid and heroic courage. The rosary has the power to change the world!

Saint Louis de Montfort, an eminent preacher of the holy rosary, stressed the importance of exercising faith when praying the rosary. He wrote:

> The holy rosary contains many mysteries of Jesus and Mary and since faith is the only key which opens up these mysteries for us, we must begin the rosary by saying the Creed very devoutly, and the stronger our faith, the more merit our rosary will have. This faith must be lively and informed by charity; in other words, to properly recite the rosary, it is necessary to be in God's grace, or at least in quest of it. This faith must be strong and constant; that is, one must not be looking for sensible devotion and spiritual consolation in the recitation of the rosary; nor should one give it up because his mind is flooded with countless involuntary distractions, or one experiences a strange distaste in the soul and an almost continual and oppressive fatigue in the body. Neither feeling, nor consolation, nor sighs, nor transports, nor the continual attention of the imagination are needed; faith and good intentions are quite enough.[1]

Faith moves mountains! The ability of the rosary to overcome evil and protect Christians, especially those in situations of extreme distress and need, has been demonstrated by countless witnesses throughout history. My own father used to tell me about how praying the rosary gave him tremendous strength and hope when he was sent to a gulag in the former Soviet Union at the end of World War II. My father's living conditions and experiences in the labor camp were cruel and painful. On a daily basis, he was required to cut down large trees in the Ural Mountains with inadequate tools, in extreme cold, and with insufficient food. Many days, he and the others who were forced into labor with him were uncertain if they would survive another day. Yet the power of the rosary was with my father in the gulag. Each morning, when he and the other men walked through the snow on their way to work, they prayed the rosary loudly together. The rosary gave them strength and hope. The praying of the rosary in those horrible circumstances was such a witness that even the Lutherans among them joined in the praying of the daily rosary. With great affection and devotion, they would all loudly pronounce the closing words of the Hail Mary: "Pray for us sinners, now and at the hour of our death. Amen!"

There has hardly been a period of human history where Christians were so systematically and cruelly persecuted as the 20th century. Sadly, though, the persecution of Christians has carried over into the 21st century. A new worldwide attack on Christianity, especially Catholicism, is occurring in every nation and culture. Evil spirits have even infiltrated the Catholic Church in our day, bringing about widespread confusion, division, and controversy. To overcome these tactics of the devil, devout Catholics in every diocese, parish, and family must gather together and pray the rosary. In this way, the snares of Lucifer can be exposed and overcome. The rosary has the power to repel the infiltrations of Satan! The rosary will protect the purity of the Catholic faith!

What are the most prominent attacks against the Church today, vicious, demonic attacks that seek to eliminate the Christian faith from the earth? They are many, but the specific forms in which they manifest themselves are the increased and orchestrated Islamization of the western world; the dictatorship of gender ideology; and the redefinition of marriage and the family. With these attacks, the Savior of the world himself is ridiculed and mocked. Yet we should not be discouraged or afraid. We possess the most powerful spiritual weapon in heaven's arsenal: the holy rosary!

With this in mind, Fr. Calloway's *10 Wonders of the Rosary* has been written to help you rediscover the spiritual power and theological richness of the rosary. Read it, reference it, and spread it around the world! I pray that this book is widely distributed and has long-lasting effects. Catholics around the world need to take up the rosary again and be fearless in holy combat against the forces of darkness!

With the rosary in our hands, we have nothing to fear.

We fight for Christ the King!

We fight for Our Lady! She conquers all heresies and we await the triumph of her Immaculate Heart!

Christus vincit!

Most Rev. Athanasius Schneider, ORC, DD
Auxiliary Bishop of the Archdiocese of Maria Santissima
Astana, Kazakhstan
October 7, 2018
(Memorial of Our Lady of the Rosary)

INTRODUCTION

In my youth, I was fascinated with the Seven Wonders of the World presented in my science and history books. The descriptions and images of the wonders made me want to travel the world and see them in person. What a disappointment it was to learn that six of the wonders had been destroyed centuries ago — the Great Pyramid of Giza, Egypt, is the only one that remains.

Today, people and organizations around the world have put together new lists of wonders. Many of these wonders are places that people can still experience firsthand. The numbers given for the wonders vary, but the lists usually provide anywhere from seven to 10 wonders. The lists include destinations where people can see such wonders as the Great Wall of China, the Grand Canyon, the Colosseum in Rome, and the Leaning Tower of Pisa. There are also lists of wonders that focus on specific aspects of nature or particular geographical regions: for example, the Seven Natural Wonders of the World; the Seven Wonders of the Underwater World; the 10 Wonders of Croatia; and so on.

In light of these lists, I thought to myself, "Why not create a list of wonders that describes some of the many fruits from one of the most beloved devotional practices in Catholicism — the rosary? It would make for a fascinating book!"

As I continued to ponder this question, I asked myself, "How many wonders does the rosary actually have? Seven? 10? 100?" In all honesty, the number is probably infinite. Yet, after much prayer and research, I discerned that 10 was a good number to focus on. Presenting 100 or more wonders of the rosary would require a book of encyclopedic proportions.

The 10 wonders presented in this book are, I believe, the most significant and important wonders of the rosary. What I love about the 10 wonders is that, unlike the majority of the Seven Wonders of the Ancient World, the 10 wonders of the rosary will never collapse, fall into ruin, or be destroyed. The 10 wonders of the rosary are everlasting and indestructible! Sure, a particular rosary may break and fall apart (it happens to my rosaries all the time), but the essence of the rosary can never be destroyed. This aspect alone makes the rosary one of the greatest wonders ever to come into existence!

As you might guess, *10 Wonders of the Rosary* has 10 chapters. Each chapter expounds on a particular wonder and contains four sections offering insights into the wonder:

1) a short story about the wonder,
2) an explanation of the wonder,
3) an example of the wonder in action, and
4) words of wonder from popes and saints.

At the end of the book, you will also find a bonus wonder and a short addendum. Hopefully, you'll agree that this whole book is short and sweet, just like the rosary itself.

I pray that this book blesses your life.

Long live the rosary in all its wonders!

Very Rev. Donald H. Calloway, MIC, STL
Vicar Provincial
Marian Fathers of the Immaculate Conception
Mary, Mother of Mercy Province

WONDER 1

THE ROSARY IS OF DIVINE ORIGIN

The origin of this form of prayer [the rosary]
is divine rather than human.[1]

Pope Leo XIII

A Woman, a Dog, and a Torch

In 12th-century Spain, a woman named Juana ("Jane" in English) experienced a most intriguing vision. She was pregnant at the time of the vision, and understood it to contain a heavenly message about the child she was bringing into the world. The woman herself was very holy. Today, she is known as Blessed Jane of Aza, and her feast day is August 2.

In 1170, Jane gave birth to a baby boy and named him Dominic. In the vision she had experienced during her pregnancy, she observed a dog leaping from her womb with a flaming torch in its mouth. The dog went all throughout the world, setting the world on fire with the torch. Unbeknownst to her at the time, her son Dominic would end up founding a religious order called the Order of Preachers (more commonly known as the Dominicans). The mission of the Dominicans would be to set the world on fire with love for Jesus through zealous preaching on the sacred mysteries of Christianity. In time, due to a play on words in Latin, the Dominicans would often be described as the *Domini canes*, the "dogs of God."

Fulfilling his mother's prophetic vision, Dominic's heavenly hounds traverse the highways and byways of the world, "sniffing" out heresy and eradicating it from the hearts and minds of the wayward. Thus, the majority of paintings of St. Dominic depict a dog with a torch in its mouth by St. Dominic's side.

One of the brightest torches to ever light up the darkness was given to the world through Blessed Jane's son: It is the divine wonder of the rosary!

Divine Origin

The rosary came into existence in the year 1208 when St. Dominic was having a tough time preaching against the errors of the Albigensians. The

Albigensians were a heretical sect that denied many of the truths of Christianity, especially those dealing with the sacred mysteries of the Life, Death, and Resurrection of Jesus Christ.

In his zeal, St. Dominic was doing his best to combat their errors and bring them back to the fold by preaching the truths of Christianity. However, after much labor and little fruit, St. Dominic retreated to a forest in southern France and prayed for divine intervention. He needed something more.

Then it happened!

According to tradition, the Mother of God appeared to him and gave him the gift of the rosary.

Chosen to be the founder of the holy rosary, St. Dominic heard the following words spoken to him by the Blessed Virgin Mary:

> Wonder not that until now you [St. Dominic] have obtained so little fruit by your labors; you have spent them on a barren soil, not yet watered with the dew of divine grace. When God willed to renew the face of the earth, he began by sending down on it the fertilizing rain of the Angelic Salutation.[2]

Mary's words to St. Dominic are reminiscent of the words spoken by the Lord to the prophet Isaiah centuries ago:

Thus says the Lord: Just as from the heavens
the rain and snow come down and do not
return there till they have watered the earth,
making it fertile and fruitful, giving seed to
the one who sows and bread to the one who
eats, so shall my word be that goes forth
from my mouth; my word shall not return
to me void, but shall do my will, achieving
the end for which I sent it (Is 55:10-11).

God's Word does not return to him void.

Knowing that St. Dominic was up against a
formidable spiritual enemy, the Queen of Heaven
gave him exactly what he needed and instructed him
further:

Dear Dominic, do you know which weapon
the Blessed Trinity wants to use to reform
the world? I want you to know that, in this
kind of warfare, the battering ram has always
been the Angelic Psalter [the Hail Mary]
which is the foundation stone of the New
Testament. Therefore, if you want to reach
these hardened souls and win them over to
God, preach my Psalter.[3]

The "Psalter" referred to by Our Lady was a
form of Marian devotion that had been in use for
several centuries. It was a simple form of devotion developed by pious monks — Cistercians and

Carthusians — that consisted of the recitation of 150 Hail Marys, but nothing more. It had no mysteries attached to it, did not involve meditation, and was not understood to be an evangelical tool or spiritual weapon.

Praying the Hail Marys of the monastic Marian Psalter was very pleasing to God and a wonderful way of honoring Mary, but God was now going to weaponize the monastic Marian Psalter, equipping it with sacred mysteries, meditations, and the zealous preaching of St. Dominic.

Accordingly, Mary told St. Dominic to combine the Our Father prayer of Jesus, the Hail Mary prayer (a combination of the words of the Archangel Gabriel to Mary and the inspired words of St. Elizabeth to the Virgin Mary), with meditation on the sacred mysteries from the Life, Death, and Resurrection of her divine Son. These mysteries, the exact same mysteries that the Albigensians were attacking, would become known as the Joyful, Sorrowful, and Glorious Mysteries of the rosary. Each 10 (or "decade of") Hail Marys would be separated by an Our Father and have a particular mystery attached to it. The new and improved, meditated and mystery-infused Marian Psalter would be a method of preaching and praying with the power to transform hearts and win back wayward souls to the fullness of the faith. The holy rosary would be an entirely new form of Marian devotion built on the foundations of the Marian Psalter, and have the power to overcome darkness and change the world!

As St. Dominic would find out, preaching, praying, and meditating on the Word of God and the sacred mysteries using the rosary was a powerful way to deliver the life-changing Word of God to people. And the Word of God has power:

> Indeed, the word of God is living and effective, sharper than any two-edged sword, penetrating even between soul and spirit, joints and marrow, and able to discern reflections and thoughts of the heart (Heb 4:12).

Some might object that the rosary can't be of divine origin, have supernatural power, and be pleasing to God because it seems to be a vain, repetitious prayer, the kind of prayer that Jesus warned us against (see Mt 6:7). However, that is incorrect. Such reasoning would convict Jesus himself of practicing *vain* repetition.

Here's what I mean.

Our Blessed Lord, as a faithful Jew, would have prayed the psalms of the Old Testament. In fact, as God, he is their primary author because the various men who wrote God's Word down were writing under the inspiration of the Holy Spirit. This means that all of Scripture is of divine origin. Speaking specifically about the psalms, there are 150 of them, and they are very repetitious (most of them containing a refrain that is constantly repeated after each stanza). But they are certainly not vain in their repetition. Praying this form of prayer is not what Jesus meant by *vain* repetition. To pray the Word of God is not vain. Remember: Jesus did this himself.

Therefore, what the psalms are for the Old Testament, the rosary is for the New Testament. The primary prayers of the rosary (Our Father and Hail Mary) come right out of the New Testament and are of divine origin. They are not man-made. Jesus would never be offended by such prayers.

Did you know that Blessed Pier Giorgio Frassati, a Third Order Dominican, always wanted his rosary to be within reach? Once, when asked if he read the Bible, he quickly responded by stating that he carried his New Testament — his rosary — in his pocket! The rosary is, indeed, a portable Bible. The rosary is the New Testament on a set of beads.

Saint Louis de Montfort put it this way:

> Just as the real thing is more important than its prefiguration, and as the body is more

than its shadow, in the same way the Psalter of Our Lady [the rosary] is greater than David's Psalter which did no more than pre-figure it [the rosary].[4]

Servant of God Sr. Lucia Dos Santos, the longest-lived visionary of the Fatima apparitions, wrote about the divine origin of the rosary, as well:

> The prayer of the rosary, after the Holy Lit-urgy of the Eucharist, is what most unites us with God by the richness of [the] prayers that compose it. All of them [the prayers of the rosary] came from heaven, dictated by the Father, by the Son, and by the Holy Spirit. The "Glory" we pray between the decades was dictated by the Father to the angels when he sent them to sing it close to his Word, the newborn child. It is also a hymn to the Trinity. The "Our Father" was dictated by the Son and it is a prayer to the Father. The "Hail Mary" is all impregnated with Trini-tarian and Eucharistic sense. The first words were dictated by the Father to the angel when he sent him to announce the mystery of the incarnation of the Word. Moved by the Holy Spirit, Saint Elizabeth said: "Blessed are thou amongst women, and blessed is the fruit of thy womb." The Church, also moved by the Holy Spirit, added, "Holy Mary, Mother of

God, pray for us sinners now and at the hour of our death."[5]

Our Lady of Las Lajas

For 800 years, God has taught his people about the divine origins of the rosary through the official writings of popes. On occasion, the Holy Trinity has also brought about miraculous events to provide further insights into how we are to understand the truthfulness of the rosary tradition as taught by popes.

In 1754, an event took place in Colombia that continues to baffle theologians, geologists, and other scientists. This event was the miraculous appearance of the image of Our Lady of Las Lajas (Our Lady of the Rocks). The image is a scientific wonder and offers strong evidence to support the heavenly origins of the rosary.

As the story goes, one day a woman named María Mueses de Quiñones was walking with her deaf and mute daughter, Rosa, through a very treacherous and rocky area on their way home from a nearby village. When a storm broke out, Maria and her daughter took shelter in the rocky cliffs of a canyon. All of a sudden, little Rosa spoke for the first time, declaring that she saw a beautiful woman who was calling her. Maria did not see or hear the woman, but was amazed that her daughter could now speak. A few days later, Rosa disappeared from the village. Her mother instinctively knew to return to the rocky canyon in order to find her little girl. Incredibly, when Maria went to the rocks, she found Rosa playing with a little child whose mother stood nearby. It was an apparition of the Virgin Mary and the Child Jesus. Maria and her daughter decided to keep this event secret, but would frequently return to the rocks to pray and ask Our Lady for her intercession.

After a few months, little Rosa suddenly fell ill and died. Distraught, Maria took her deceased daughter to the rocks to ask Our Lady to intercede with her Son to bring Rosa back to life. Miraculously, Rosa came back to life. When Maria returned to the village and the people saw that Rosa was alive, their interest was piqued about this place where little Rosa had miraculously recovered her speech and even come back from death. The villagers followed Maria and Rosa to the rocks to see the place themselves. While they were there, someone noticed a beautiful image of Our Lady on the rocks. Neither Maria nor Rosa had seen the image there before. No one knew who had painted it or where it had come from. In the beautiful image, Our Lady is holding the Child Jesus and handing St. Dominic a rosary; the Child Jesus is extending a friar's cord to St. Francis of Assisi.

After an investigation, civil authorities and scientists determined that the scene was not a painting at all. Miraculously, the image is part of the rock itself. Geologists have since bored core samples from several places in the rock and discovered that there is no paint, dye, or pigment on the surface of the rock. The colors of the mysterious image are the colors of the rock itself, and extend several feet deep inside the rock! The only man-made aspects of the miraculous image are the crowns above the heads of Jesus and Mary, later added by local devotees. For more than two centuries, the location has been a place of pilgrimage and devotion. In 1951, the Church authorized devotion to Our Lady under the title of "Our Lady of Las Lajas," and the church built around the image has been declared a minor basilica.

WORDS OF WONDER

We consider the holy rosary the most convenient and most fruitful means [to obtain the aid of Mary], as is clearly suggested by the very origin of this practice, heavenly rather than human.[6]

Venerable Pope Pius XII

The rosary is pleasing to the Blessed Virgin because of its origin and its excellence. In fact, the rosary is not the product of human fancy; it was suggested to men by the Blessed Virgin herself, and she had the most sublime purpose for doing so. Mary personally gave us this precious token of salvation, and she also taught us the manner of using it.[7]

Blessed James Alberione

The whole Catholic world eagerly received the holy rosary, and innumerable graces and miracles of conversion testified to its supernatural origin.[8]

St. Maximilian Kolbe

WONDER 2

THE ROSARY IS A
SPIRITUAL WEAPON

*I could conquer the world if I had
an army to say the rosary.*[1]

Blessed Pope Pius IX

A Polish Pope and a Lightsaber

The rosary was given by Our Lady to St. Dominic to be used as a spiritual weapon against the falsehoods of his time.

Today, there are new falsehoods threatening the sacred mysteries of Christianity. To respond to these threats, the Mother of God chose another holy priest, a pope, to wield the spiritual weapon and combat the errors of his time. Modern falsehoods require ancient truths to answer them, and this holy pontiff re-sharpened, renewed, and reloaded the ancient weapon!

In 1978, to the amazement of the entire world, the first non-Italian since 1523 was elected to the papacy. He was Cardinal Karol Wojtyla, a humble and holy prelate from Krakow, Poland. He took the name John Paul II, and within two weeks of the start of his pontificate, he announced to the entire world that the rosary was his favorite prayer!

As a young man, he had been a member of the Association of the Living Rosary and prayed the rosary every day. He had endured the horrors of Communism, Socialism, and Nazism, and knew that the rosary was a weapon against all falsehoods.

As the Vicar of Christ on earth, he decided to offer the Church a "new" set of mysteries that would combat modern errors: the Luminous Mysteries.

By this action, he transformed the ancient sword of the rosary into a modern-day lightsaber.

Each of the five Luminous Mysteries sheds light on the darkness of modern-day falsehoods and offers a mystery of light for people to contemplate: the importance of Baptism, the sanctity of Marriage, the need for conversion, the Divinity of Christ, and the Real Presence of Jesus Christ in the Holy Eucharist.

The rosary is ready to meet the challenges of the 21st century!

Spiritual Weapon

Did you notice that there were quotes placed around the word "new" when the Luminous Mysteries of St. John Paul II were mentioned in the previous section?

There's a reason, and you need to know it.

As amazing as St. John Paul II was — and, in my opinion, he was one of the best popes to ever hold the office of Vicar of Christ — he is technically not the inventor of the Luminous Mysteries.

Say what?

You probably didn't know that, did you? The Church is extremely grateful to St. John Paul II for offering us the Luminous Mysteries in his 2002 apostolic letter *Rosarium Virginis Mariae* (*The Rosary of the Blessed Virgin Mary*), but the reality is that if we do a little historical research, we will quickly find that he did not invent them. They have been a long time in the making.

Unbeknownst to most people, it was St. George Preca (a holy priest from the island of Malta) who proposed a new set of mysteries called the "Mysteries of Light" in 1957. The mysteries he desired to see promoted were the same five mysteries that St. John Paul II used to sharpen the blade of the rosary 45 years later in his 2002 apostolic letter on the rosary, a letter that essentially transformed the rosary into a modern day lightsaber.

Why is this important? Sadly, there are some people who believe that the Luminous Mysteries are merely the invention of the post-Vatican II Church, without legitimacy. They consider the "new" mysteries to be a corruption of the original, true rosary. This is most unfortunate. The Luminous Mysteries are a gift to the Church for our times, weapons given from heaven to combat modern errors. The Luminous Mysteries did not come into existence after the Second Vatican Council. The reason that the majority of the Church "missed" learning about the true origins of the Luminous Mysteries is simply that George Preca was beatified four months before the terrorist attacks on September 11, 2001. Because the entire focus of the world was on what happened on 9/11, the Church and the world didn't get a chance to learn about the history of the Luminous Mysteries.

Even before this, however, there were others throughout history who sought to promote new meditations and mysteries for the rosary (for example, St. Louis de Montfort and Venerable Patrick Peyton, among others). However, it was specifically the Luminous Mysteries of St. George Preca that St. John Paul II officially embraced and promoted.

Wait. "Saint" George Preca? Isn't he just a Blessed?

Nope: The founder of the Luminous Mysteries was canonized by Pope Benedict XVI in 2007!

As did St. George Preca and St. John Paul II, some of the greatest Marian saints have presented the rosary as a spiritual weapon for the faithful. In fact, from the very beginning, the rosary has been understood as a weapon because it was given to the world during a time of knights, chivalry, and swords.

Shortly after the rosary was given to the world, the Dominicans and members of other mendicant religious orders began to wear the rosary on the left side of their habit in imitation of knights. Most people are right-handed, and knights would wear their sword on their left side for easy access when drawing the sword out of its sheath. Even today, in practically every religious order that has a rosary as part of their habit, the rosary is usually worn by the religious on their left side to signify that it is a spiritual sword.

In the 15th century, Blessed Alan de la Roche, a Dominican, brought about a greater awareness of the rosary among the faithful. He conducted much research on the power of the Hail Mary prayer in order to write books about the rosary. In his research, he discovered that St. Albert the Great, a Dominican, Doctor of the Church, and teacher of St. Thomas Aquinas, had given a homily about the marvels of the Hail Mary prayer. One of the most powerful statements he found in the homily was when St. Albert spoke of the connection between the Hail Mary and being equipped for spiritual combat. Saint Albert said:

> The eighth [marvel of the Hail Mary] is that it is the mine of all metals, thanks to which you are enriched and able to construct weapons to defend yourself against all enemies.[2]

Saint Louis de Montfort, a Third Order Dominican, wrote *The Secret of the Rosary*, the greatest book ever written on the rosary. He considered the Hail Mary prayed during the rosary to be sword-like, as well. He wrote:

> The Hail Mary is a sharp and flaming shaft which, joined to the Word of God, gives the preacher the strength to pierce, move, and convert the most hardened hearts.[3]

Saint Padre Pio referred to the rosary as his spiritual weapon. He wielded it (that is, he prayed it) dozens of times a day. He always told others that the rosary is the weapon that wins all spiritual battles.

Saint Teresa of Calcutta, too, almost always held a rosary in her hand. Once, when she was going through a security checkpoint in an airport, the airport guards asked if anyone was bringing any weapons through the checkpoint. To the surprise of everyone, St. Teresa raised her hand and said she had a weapon! Opening her hand, she revealed to everyone present her rosary.

Saint Maximilian Kolbe, founder of the Militia Immaculatae, instructed all the members of his spiritual militia to wield the spiritual sword of the rosary.

Popes and saints have often described the rosary in warlike terms.

Blessed Columba Marmion and Venerable Pope Pius XII considered the rosary to be a weapon similar to the sling of David from the Old Testament (see 1 Sam 17). As the tiny pebbles of the sling of David brought down the mighty Goliath, the tiny beads of the rosary slay the giants of darkness present in the world today.

Blessed James Alberione, the founder of the Daughters of St. Paul, also compared the rosary to David's sling, saying:

> With this mighty weapon she [Mary] has defeated Satan, just as with a sling David defeated the giant Goliath.[4]

Several very holy priests of the 20th century have even described the rosary using metaphors of modern weaponry.

The Servant of God Joseph Kentenich, founder of the Schoenstatt movement, said:

> The rosary is a sort of machine gun and atomic bomb, namely a weapon that is far superior to all the weapons of modern warfare in overcoming the enemy of God.[5]

The Servant of God Dolindo Ruotolo, a very holy priest from Naples, Italy, whom St. Padre Pio considered a saint, said something similar:

> The rosary is a powerful prayer against Satan and against the assaults of evil. Our Church brought, and continues to bring, great triumphs because of this prayer. The decades of the rosary, from this point of view, are like the belt of a machine gun: every bead is a shot, every affection of the soul is as an explosion of faith that frightens off Satan, and Mary once more crushes his head.[6]

Powerful words! The saints know what they are talking about; we should listen to them.

Lastly, lest someone claim that referring to the rosary in such militant terms is outdated and no modern pontiff would refer to the rosary in this way, the words of a 21ˢᵗ-century pope should put the question to rest. Pope Benedict XVI, during a 2008 pastoral visit to the Pontifical Shrine of Our Lady of the Rosary in Pompeii, Italy, stated:

> The rosary is a spiritual weapon in the battle against evil, against all violence, for peace in hearts, in families, in society, and in the world.[7]

The Great Siege of Malta

In the 16ᵗʰ century, the Protestant rebellion caused Christianity to be divided. Men who worshipped the same God began to fight against one another, and entire nations turned their backs on the one true Church founded by Jesus Christ: the Catholic Church. While this was happening, another religion sought to take advantage of Christian division: Islam. Its intention was to conquer Christianity by means of the powerful Turkish Ottoman Empire.

When Suleiman the Magnificent became the leader of the Muslims in the middle of the 16ᵗʰ century, he expressed an outright hatred for Christianity. His grandfather had once made a vow that he would not rest until he had stabled his horses beneath the dome of St. Peter's and wound the head of the pope with a turban. Suleiman desired to carry out the dream of his grandfather and envisioned the Vatican as a red apple ready to be plucked and plundered for Allah. The center of Christianity was under real threat from Muslim invaders. Indeed, the very fate of Western Civilization was at risk.

In the previous century, Muslims had already taken over Constantinople, the center of Christianity in the east for centuries. When the Muslims captured Constantinople in 1453, they renamed it "Istanbul" and turned its greatest Byzantine church, Hagia Sophia, into a mosque.

In 1565, the powerful Ottoman Empire inched closer to Rome. To conquer Rome and turn St. Peter's into a mosque would be a major defeat for Christianity. The Muslims knew that in order to get to Rome via the sea, they had to capture the strategic island of Malta. Their attempt to take the island is known as the Great Siege of Malta.

In this siege, the Muslim armada consisted of more than 40,000 men, while the Catholic army consisted of only about 6,000 men. The odds were greatly against the Catholics. Miraculously, under the leadership of Jean Parisot de Valette, the grand master of the Sovereign Military Order of St. John (the Knights of Malta), the Catholic army was able to defend the island and repel the Muslims. While the Catholic army suffered many casualties, the Muslim army suffered the loss of more than 30,000 men.

The most fascinating aspect of the Great Siege of Malta involves the sword used by Jean Parisot de Valette during the battle. In preparation for the confrontation with the Muslims, de Valette went to a blacksmith and commissioned a special sword. He requested that a rosary be engraved on the blade of his sword! He knew what the rosary was, and he wasn't afraid to show it in battle. The rosary was his spiritual weapon!

After the battle was won, de Valette made a pilgrimage to the famous icon of Our Lady of Damascus in Birgu, Malta (a town also known as Vittoriosa), and laid his cap and sword at the feet of Our Lady's image. The sword, as well as the cap, remain on display to this day in the small museum attached to the Catholic church dedicated to Our Lady of Damascus in Birgu.

WORDS OF WONDER

As St. Dominic employed this prayer [the rosary] as a sword to destroy the monstrous heresy of the Albigensians, so likewise in our time the faithful, in using the same weapon — that is to say, the daily recitation of the rosary — will obtain that, by the all-powerful protection of the Mother of God, the many errors infecting the world will be uprooted and destroyed.[8]

Blessed Pope Pius IX

Today, as in other times, the rosary must be a powerful weapon to enable us to win in our interior struggle, and to help all souls.[9]

St. Josemaría Escrivá

When combined with the pure contemplative prayer of the rosary meditations, the Hail Mary becomes the most powerful weapon ever placed in the hands of man — a weapon which, through God and his most blessed Mother, will someday change the face of the earth.[10]

Venerable Patrick Peyton

WONDER 3

THE ROSARY IS
FEARED BY SATAN

*The devils have an overwhelming
fear of the rosary.*[1]

St. Louis de Montfort

Saint Dominic and 15,000 Demons

In *The Secret of the Rosary*, St. Louis de Montfort recounts the following story about what happened when St. Dominic encountered a man possessed by 15,000 demons:

> While St. Dominic was preaching the rosary in Carcassone [France], a heretic made fun of the miracles and the fifteen mysteries of the holy rosary [this was before the Luminous Mysteries], and this prevented other heretics from being converted. As a punishment, God suffered fifteen thousand devils to enter

the man's body. His parents took him to Father Dominic to be delivered from the evil spirits. He [St. Dominic] started to pray and begged everyone who was there to say the rosary out loud with him, and at each Hail Mary Our Lady drove one hundred devils out of the heretic's body and they came out in the form of red hot coals.[2]

Demons have a tremendous fear of the rosary. Saint Dominic knew this, and so he employed the rosary as a form of exorcism. Our Lady had taught the founder of the rosary that in order to overcome the devil, he needed to fight fire with fire. The rosary is divine fire!

Saint Bonaventure once put it this way:

As wax melts before fire, so do the devils lose their power against those souls who remember the name of Mary and devoutly invoke it.[3]

Feared by Satan

Do you believe in dragons?

You should.

Not the Komodo dragons of Indonesia. Those are the kind people can see, and everyone acknowledges their existence. It's the kind of dragons that can't be seen that many people no longer believe are real. If only people knew that, in the Bible, Satan is referred to as a dragon (see Rev 12:9), perhaps they would take the threat he poses more seriously and use the rosary-sword to defeat him.

Allow me to explain.

The bookends of human history (Genesis and Revelation) speak of a woman and her offspring conquering and crushing a serpent dragon (see Gen 3:15; Rev 12).

The Catholic Church has always understood the woman to be the Blessed Virgin Mary; her offspring, Jesus Christ; and the serpent dragon, Lucifer. What is often overlooked, however, is that the story involving Jesus, Mary, and the dragon also involves a sword.

With the fall of Adam and Eve, the Holy Bible tells us that God "placed before the paradise of pleasure cherubims, and a flaming sword, turning every way, to keep the way of the tree of life" (Gen 3:24). This is most interesting! What does it mean?

We don't know much about the sword, other than that the Bible states that it prevented Adam, Eve, and their descendants from having access to paradise. No man, woman, or child could touch it or take hold of it, let alone wield it. The flaming sword apparently worked in the devils' favor by keeping mankind out of paradise. After all, Satan doesn't want men and women to be with God.

But doesn't God want us to be with him in paradise? And aren't all swords meant to be held by someone and wielded against an enemy? The answer to both questions is a strong "Yes!"

What was hidden from the devil — and from the world, too — was that our heavenly Father had a plan. His plan would be manifested "in the fullness of time" (see Gal 4:4-5) when his Word became flesh and took on human nature. Through the Incarnation, the God-Man would have the ability — unlike us — to take hold of the sword and wield it against the serpent dragon. As Savior of the world, Jesus Christ shares the ability to wield this sword with us, weak and fallen creatures. We would have the power to slay the dragon! The sword that had prevented us from coming near the tree of life and eating its fruit was now in the hands of Jesus Christ. He infused into it the sacred mysteries of his Life, Death, and Resurrection and handed it on to us.

Nobody slays a dragon without a sword!

The devil never saw this coming. God tricked him. The very thing that had kept us out of paradise

— and that the dragon had used against us — is now the very thing we use to slay the serpent and enter paradise!

Saint Ignatius of Antioch, a bishop and martyr from the early Church, was on to something when he noted the following about God's secret and hidden plan, a plan that involved sacred mysteries:

> Mary's virginity and her giving birth escaped the notice of the prince of this world, as did the Lord's death — those three secrets crying to be told, but wrought in God's silence.[4]

The mysteries of the God-Man were wrought in silence, but now they are crying to be told!

So, what about the sword? What is it?

Well, it could be that the sword is a symbol of the Catholic Church. To be clear, the Catholic Church did not yet exist when Adam and Eve were banished from the garden and the flaming sword was erected to keep them out. However, this does not mean that God didn't have the Catholic Church in mind when all of this happened. In other words, the Catholic Church was not an afterthought in the mind of God, any more than the Incarnation of Jesus Christ wasn't an afterthought. On the contrary, both the Incarnation of the Word (Jesus Christ) and the establishment of his Mystical Body, the Catholic

Church, were intended by God from the beginning. Jesus would overcome the dragon and *hand on* to the members of his Mystical Body the sacred mysteries, the flaming sword, that conquers the dragon and allows access to heaven. In this sense, the sword can be seen as a symbol of the Catholic Church.

So what has this to do with the rosary?

Something wonderful!

Again, from a spiritual perspective, it could be that the flaming sword is also symbolic of the sword of the rosary that God would one day give to the Catholic Church. When the rosary-sword was given to the world in the year 1208, nothing new was added to the teaching or doctrine of the Church. What God gave to the Church through the rosary was a new method of prayer for defeating the devil.

The serpent dragon knew exactly what it meant, too, and it enraged him.

For 1,200 years, the Catholic Church had been teaching and preaching the sacred mysteries of Jesus Christ to the faithful on Sundays and Solemnities. With the advent of the rosary, however, an entirely new way of praying was given to the world. It would turn every Christian home into a domestic church and catechetical school. The rosary would give all people, clergy and laity, the ability to wield the sword and slay the dragon on a daily basis.

Praying the rosary does not require literacy or prestige. The uneducated, the poor, and the young can all pray the rosary with the same powerful effect as bishops, priests, and nuns. The rosary flows from the doctrine and Sacraments of the Church, and leads back to the doctrine and Sacraments of the Church. For this reason — and many more — the devil knew that when God gave the rosary to the world, the Catholic Church would effectively launch a worldwide catechetical campaign.

Satan knows what the sword of sacred mysteries is capable of doing. The rosary-sword has the power to cut off the seven deadly heads of the ancient serpent — the sins of pride, lust, gluttony, greed, sloth, wrath, and envy. The devil had been striving to destroy the Catholic Church since its inception. Therefore, he went on the attack against the new form of prayer given to the world in the rosary. It didn't take long before the dragon set fire to the earth in an attempt to rid the world of the divine weapon.

Did you know that in the 14th century — the century after the rosary was founded — a plague killed one third of the population of Europe? Historians have estimated that more than 25 million people died. Saint Louis de Montfort believed that the reason for the Black Plague of the 14th century was the wicked scheming and jealousy of the devil, which led him to try to get rid of the rosary that had only been founded in the previous century by St. Dominic.

Satan knows that the rosary has a divine origin, and he knows that it is indestructible. Since he can't destroy it directly, he constantly seeks to eliminate it in other ways. He burns historical evidence, destroys documents and artwork associated with the rosary, and casts doubts in the hearts of priests regarding its power and heavenly origins. When there are new forms of devotion given to the world that use rosary beads (for example, the Divine Mercy Chaplet), he tries to destroy the new messages and burn all documentation associated with them.

Saint Padre Pio, one of the greatest mystics of the 20th century, knew well how much the devil hates the rosary and said the following:

> Satan always tries to destroy this prayer [the rosary], but he will never succeed. It is the prayer of her who triumphs over everything and everyone.[5]

Sister Lucia Dos Santos also knew how much the devil hates the rosary. She understood that the devil is waging a constant battle against this devotion because the rosary offers tremendous light to souls. She wrote:

> The simple remembrance of the mysteries in each decade is another radiance of light supporting the smoking torch of souls. This is why the devil has moved against it such a great war.[6]

Satan fears the doctrine and Sacraments of the Catholic Church. He also fears the sacred mysteries of Jesus Christ prayed on the blessed beads of Our Lady.

One day, the God-Man will use this sword to deliver the final blow to the dragon, as the prophet Isaiah foretold:

> In that day, the Lord will punish with his sword — his fierce, great, and powerful sword — Leviathan the gliding serpent, Leviathan the coiling serpent; he will slay the dragon in the sea (Is 27:1).

A Serial Killer vs. the Rosary

In 1978, the rosary saved a young woman from being raped and killed by the infamous serial killer Ted Bundy. Responsible for at least 30 brutal and sadistic murders, Ted Bundy was eventually caught and executed by electric chair in 1989. Before his death, he testified to an aspect of one of his killing sprees in Florida that not even he understood.

On the evening of January 15, 1978, Bundy broke into a sorority house at Florida State University in Tallahassee and brutally assaulted and killed several young women. However, one of the women in the house remained completely untouched, even though she had come face-to-face with the killer. When police arrived at the scene of the brutal murders, they found the young woman in a near-catatonic state, unwilling to speak to anyone but a priest. A local priest, Monsignor William Kerr, was called to the scene to speak to the woman. She told him that after Ted Bundy had killed two of her sorority sisters and severely harmed two others, he opened the door to her room, ready to kill her. Oddly, when Bundy opened the door and saw her lying in bed, he dropped his weapon and ran away. The young woman told Msgr. Kerr that before she had gone off to college, she had promised her mother that every night before going to bed, she would pray a rosary for protection. That particular night, she had fallen asleep while praying the rosary. The rosary was in her hand when Bundy opened the door and looked at her.

Incredibly, when Ted Bundy was on death row, he asked for spiritual guidance from Msgr. William

Kerr, the same priest that had talked to the young woman on the night of the murders. In the course of their conversation, Bundy informed Msgr. Kerr that he had no idea why he had not killed the young woman. He said that when he had gotten to her room, he had had every intention of killing her, but a mysterious force prevented him from entering the room, and he dropped his weapon and fled. He didn't know it, but that mysterious force was the rosary!

WORDS OF WONDER

Let victory be thine, O Mother. Thou wilt conquer. Yes, thou hast the power to overcome all heresies, errors, and vice. And I, confident in your powerful protection, will engage in the battle, not only against flesh and blood, but against the prince of darkness, as the Apostle [Paul] says, grasping the shield of the holy rosary and armed with the double-edged sword of the divine word.[7]

St. Anthony Mary Claret

When people say the rosary together it is far more formidable to the devil than one said privately, because in this public prayer it is an army that is attacking him. He can often overcome the prayer of an individual, but if this prayer is joined to that of other Christians, the devil has much more trouble in getting the best of it. It is very easy to break a single stick, but if you join it to others to make a bundle it cannot be broken.[8]

St. Louis de Montfort

The Mother of God, the Virgin most powerful, who in times past co-operated in charity that the faithful might be born in the Church, is now the intermediary, the Mediatrix of our salvation. May she shatter and strike off the multiple heads of the wicked hydra.[9]

Pope Leo XIII

WONDER 4

THE ROSARY CROWNS MARY WITH SPIRITUAL ROSES

Christians have the praiseworthy practice of offering each day with great devotion the crown of Marian roses to their beloved Mother.[1]

St. Anthony Mary Claret

Mother's Day

Honoring one's mother is pleasing to God. Celebrations in honor of motherhood date back to ancient times, especially in Greek and Roman cultures. Today, almost every culture has some kind of observance giving tribute to mothers, and most of these celebrations involve flowers.

In 1908, Anna Marie Jarvis began an initiative in the United States to have created an annual holiday honoring motherhood and mothers. The first

Mother's Day was celebrated in Grafton, West Virginia, on May 10, 1908. A few years later, all other states began celebrating this special day on the second Sunday in May, the month of flowers.

In the Judeo-Christian tradition, honoring your mother fulfills one of the Ten Commandments (see Ex 20:12). In the New Testament, one of the greatest gifts that Jesus gives to his disciples is the gift of his mother. He shared her motherhood with us when he said from the Cross: "Woman, behold your son!" (Jn 19:26).

Catholics show their love for their spiritual mother in a very special way when they pray the rosary. To pray the rosary is to crown Mary's head with beautiful heavenly roses! Blessed William Joseph Chaminade expressed this wonder very succinctly. He wrote:

> The rosary is like a crown of roses, like a diadem with which the faithful decorate the head of their queen.[2]

Saint Anthony Mary Claret noted what many saints and scholars have done on a daily basis to honor Mary, their spiritual mother:

> The ancient peoples of the East had a practice of offering rose-wreaths to be worn as

crowns to distinguished persons; and true Christians have the praiseworthy practice of offering each day with great devotion the crown of Marian roses to their beloved Mother, the Blessed Virgin. Such was the practice of St. Louis King of France, the great Bossuet, Fenelon, St. Vincent de Paul, St. Charles Borromeo, St. Francis de Sales, St. Francis Xavier, and others.[3]

The rosary makes every day Mother's Day!

Spiritual Roses

From its beginning, the rosary was understood by St. Dominic to be *both* a spiritual weapon and a way of crowning Mary, our spiritual mother, with heavenly roses. In my book *Champions of the Rosary: The History and Heroes of a Spiritual Weapon*, I present documentary evidence that the word "rosary" was in use during the century of St. Dominic. Even then, it was used as a way of describing St. Dominic's new form of prayer. In fact, Pope Urban IV (pope from 1261–1264) used the word "rosary" and offered indulgences to the faithful who prayed it.

Nevertheless, the word "rosary" did not become the universally accepted term to describe St. Dominic's method of praying the Marian Psalter until the 15th century. The specific event that helped bring about the name change did not occur until 1422.

Saint Maximilian Kolbe offers an excellent historical account of how the change came about:

> Originally the rosary was called the Psalter of Mary, because as the Davidic Psalter is composed of 150 psalms, so also in the rosary we find 150 Hail Marys. The following circumstance, according to its application, contributed to the name change: A pious young man [a Franciscan novice, in the year 1422] had a habit of frequently adorning an image of the Blessed Virgin Mary with roses. He later joined a monastery. Within the walls of the monastery, he no longer had the opportunity to bring flowers to Mary; this grieved him very much. While he was afflicted in this way, the Blessed Virgin Mary appeared to him and said: "Recite devoutly my psalter, and adorn me with the most beautiful flowers." He began therefore to pray the rosary, and immediately he saw how for each Hail Mary the Blessed Virgin Mary took forth from his mouth a rose of wondrous beauty and weaved with those roses a garland for herself. At the Our Father she wove into the garland a resplendent lily. This was the origin of the name "Rosary."[4]

According to the apparition of the Virgin Mary to the Franciscan novice, the Marian Psalter and the rosary are the exact same thing. This had been true ever since the time of St. Dominic, when Our Lady had weaponized the Marian Psalter with sacred mysteries and meditation. Mary's appearance to the pious young man was meant to inform him that by praying the meditated Marian Psalter (aka the rosary), he would be able to continue his pious practice of crowning Mary with spiritual roses, just as he had been doing before joining the monastery.

Another fascinating aspect of the apparition to the Franciscan novice is that, according to the Franciscan tradition, Mary also gave the novice a type of rosary particular to the Franciscan Order. This rosary is known as the Franciscan Corona (or Crown) rosary. In the Franciscan Crown rosary, the person who prays it meditates on seven joys of Mary (the Annunciation, Visitation, Nativity of Jesus, Adoration of the Magi, Finding in the Temple, the Resurrection, and either the Assumption of Mary or the Coronation of Mary).

It was after the 1422 apparition to the Franciscan novice that the word "rosary" became the universally accepted way of describing all Marian Psalters — not only the traditional Dominican rosary, but also the

Rosary of the Seven Sorrows of Mary promoted by the Servites; the Brigittine rosary founded by St. Bridget of Sweden; and the Carmelite rosary. Mary's apparition to the Franciscan novice was intended to remind the entire Church, not only the pious young Franciscan, that all meditated Marian Psalters — rosaries — are a way of crowning her with heavenly roses.

You may be wondering, "How did the world ever forget this fundamental dimension of the rosary devotion?" It's a good question, and one that has an answer.

In short, the first meditated Marian Psalter — the Dominican rosary — had been almost entirely forgotten during the Black Plague of the 14th century. At the time of the plague, most people forgot about the rosary and its significance because they were more preoccupied with survival and the preservation of life. Remember: One third of the population of Europe died during the Black Plague, and most of the original documents on the rosary and its meaning were burned because they were housed in contaminated buildings.

When Mary appeared to the Franciscan novice in 1422, she reminded him — and the Church — that the rosary was a way of crowning her with spiritual roses. This helped bring about the name change from psalter to rosary. Then, at the end of the 15th century, when a zealous son of St. Dominic, Blessed Alan de la Roche, reestablished the original rosary and its Confraternity, the entire Church began to refer to the Marian Psalter of St. Dominic as *the* rosary. Incidentally, in 1980, Mary appeared to an older gentleman in Cuapa, Nicaragua, and showed him a history of the rosary that is in complete agreement with what has been written above. The Cuapa apparition has been approved by the local bishop in Nicaragua. (See the Addendum on page 147 for a detailed description of this event.)

Saint Louis de Montfort wrote about the name change, as well. In *The Secret of the Rosary,* he notes:

> Ever since Blessed Alan de la Roche reestablished this devotion [the Marian Psalter], the voice of the people, which is the voice of God, called it the rosary. The word rosary means "Crown of Roses." Being heavenly flowers, these roses will never fade or lose their exquisite beauty.[5]

What mother would not want to receive roses from her children? To receive such a gift from a child would delight any mother's heart.

Praying the rosary devotion gives us the ability to crown our spiritual mother with beautiful spiritual roses. To do this, you don't have to be the pope, a priest, or a nun. No money is required, and you don't have to be an eloquent speaker, well-known, or even educated. All that is needed is a desire to offer a spiritual bouquet to your heavenly mother.

Such gifts to Mary would never offend Jesus, either. How could they?

Think about it: You have an earthly mother. You love her. If someone were to ask you if it would be okay if they gave your mother roses, your heart would be moved. In all probability, you would be delighted by such a token of honor given to your mother. You would be an odd son or daughter if you were offended by such a gesture. The person who did this for your mom would have your attention, and you would most likely consider them a dear friend. If you were able, you might even give them certain privileges and favors in return. Honor given to your mother would make you very happy.

Why would it be any different for Jesus?

Jesus is the Son of Mary. He loves her very much. He loves her more than we ever could. He will never be offended if we crown his mother with roses by praying Hail Marys and meditating on his sacred mysteries. To think otherwise would be an insult to his love for his mother.

Those who have a deep prayer life understand this. Those who have a deep prayer life understand that love is at the heart of the rosary.

Saint John Paul II, a man deeply in love with Jesus and Mary, put it this way:

> To understand the rosary, one has to enter into the psychological dynamic proper to love.[6]

What the great Polish pope was getting at is that when you love someone, you never tire of telling them you love them. Saying "I love you" to your mother would never be considered an offense or vain repetition. It can be done a million times, and yet it is always fresh and new.

Saying "I love you" to Jesus and Mary is exactly what we do when we pray the rosary.

Venerable Fulton J. Sheen expressed it this way:

> When we say the rosary — we are saying to God, the Trinity, to the Incarnate Savior, to the Blessed Mother: "I love you, I love you, I love you."[7]

Fulton Sheen was so in love with Mary that he always made a point of including the rosary when he taught catechism. On one occasion, he encountered a lady who was very much opposed to praying the rosary. His response was to show her that the rosary is grounded in love. He wrote:

> A woman came to see me one evening after instruction. She said, "I would never become a Catholic. You say the same words in the rosary over and over again, and anyone who repeats the same words is never sincere. I would never believe anyone who repeated his words, and neither would God." I asked her who the man was with her. She said he was her fiancé. I asked: "Does he love you?" "Certainly, he does." "But how do you know?" "He told me." "What did he say?" "He said: 'I love you.'" "When did he tell you last?" "About an hour ago." "Did he tell you before?" "Yes, last night. He tells me every night." I said: "Don't believe him. He is repeating; he is not sincere."[8]

Love is the answer. Love is what the rosary is all about.

Love your spiritual mother. Crown her every day by praying the rosary.

In Catholicism, every day is Mother's Day!

The Battle of Muret

The first rosary victory was won at the Battle of Muret on September 12, 1213 (the Feast of the Holy Name of Mary). At that battle, the rosary was understood to be *both* a spiritual weapon *and* a way of crowning Mary with heavenly roses.

A small town in southern France near the city of Toulouse, Muret was a stronghold for a group of Albigensian heretics. The pope at the time, Innocent III, was deeply concerned about their expansion, and sought to organize a Crusader army that would rid France of their heretical influence once and for all. With the pope's blessing, a Catholic force was assembled in southern France by Count Simon de Montfort. Unfortunately, the army only consisted of 1,500 men. Count Simon had hoped for reinforcements from northern France, but they never arrived. The Albigensian forces, on the other hand, had more than 30,000 men, led by Raymond of Toulouse and Pedro II of Aragon. Theirs was a voracious group of warmongers with one goal in mind: Wipe out the puny Catholic militia. Confident in their greater numbers, the Albigensian army was convinced that they would crush the opposing Catholic force. Believing they were invincible, the

Albigensian army spent the night before the battle in drunkenness and debauchery — an error that would prove to be their downfall.

In contrast, the entire Catholic army, under the joint command of Count Simon de Montfort and St. Dominic, spent the night before the battle praying the rosary. In the early hours of the morning, Holy Mass was celebrated for the Catholic militia, and many men went to Confession. Saint Dominic retreated to the Church of Saint-Jacques in Muret to pray for victory.

Sure enough, in the time it took St. Dominic to pray a rosary, Simon de Montfort and his men were able to rush upon the hung-over and disorganized Albigensians and completely rout them. The Albigensian army never saw it coming. Chroniclers and historians who recorded the events of the battle described the routing of the Albigensian militia as the felling of many trees under the axes of an army of lumberjacks. With the complete triumph of the Catholic forces, the territorial expansion of the Albigensian heresy ended.

After the battle, every Catholic in the area attributed the victory to the rosary. Simon de Montfort and the local people even constructed a chapel dedicated to the rosary in the Church of St. Jacques where St.

Dominic had been praying during the battle — the first chapel ever to be dedicated to the rosary. A painting that depicted the Blessed Virgin giving the rosary to St. Dominic was enshrined in the chapel.

In early 1214, less than one year after the battle, a notary of Languedoc (formerly a small province in southern France) wrote a poem describing how St. Dominic brought roses to the battle, offered them repeatedly, and made a wreath out of them. This, of course, was a poetic reference to the praying of Hail Marys by St. Dominic during the battle.

A weapon and a rose. That's what the rosary has always been.

WORDS OF WONDER

Our Lady has shown her thorough approval of the name Rosary; she has revealed to several people that each time they say a Hail Mary they are giving her a beautiful rose and that each complete rosary makes her a crown of roses.[9]

St. Louis de Montfort

Blessed are we if we are faithful in reciting that very popular and splendid prayer — the rosary — which is a kind of measured spelling out of our feelings of affection in the invocation: Hail Mary, Hail Mary, Hail Mary. Our life will be a fortunate one if it is interwoven with this garland of roses, with this circlet of praise to Mary, to the mysteries of her Divine Son.[10]

St. Pope Paul VI

The Marian rosary is a marvelous garland woven from the angelic annunciation interspersed with the Lord's Prayer and joined together with a course of meditation, a most efficacious kind of entreaty, and most especially fruitful for the attainment of everlasting life. For this reason, in addition to the most excellent prayers of which it is comprised and which are, as it were, plaited into a crown of heavenly roses, it also offers an invitation to stir up one's faith, a help to devotion, and outstanding models of virtue through the mysteries presented for contemplation. It therefore cannot fail to be most pleasing to the Virgin Mother of God and to her only Son, who undoubtedly considers any praise, honor, and glory rendered to his mother as likewise rendered to himself.[11]

Venerable Pope Pius XII

WONDER 5

THE ROSARY BRINGS ABOUT CONVERSION

If you wish to convert anyone to the fullness of the knowledge of Our Lord and of his Mystical Body, then teach him the rosary.[1]

Venerable Fulton J. Sheen

A Devilish Italian Lawyer

In the 19th century in Naples, Italy, a young man named Bartolo Longo left home to go to college to study and become a lawyer. Bartolo had been raised Catholic, but in Italy at that time, there was a very strong nationalist movement sweeping through the universities. The movement ridiculed the teachings of the Catholic Church and considered them old wives' tales. As a result, Bartolo abandoned the Catholicism of his youth and looked for meaning in life by attending séances with various cults. He was so enamored by the practices of the occult that he became an ordained priest of Satan!

The fruit of his involvement in the occult was that he began to suffer nightmares, hallucinations, major depression, and very serious anxiety attacks. He thought his involvement in the occult would lead to a meaningful life and happiness, but the opposite happened. Things got so bad that he even contemplated suicide.

At his wits' end, Bartolo broke down and went to talk to a Catholic priest. The priest he talked to was Fr. Alberto Radente, a Dominican priest and a great promoter of the rosary. Father Radente told Bartolo about the power of the rosary and the promises that Mary had once given to St. Dominic and Bl. Alan de la Roche. Bartolo knew that this was his way out of the occult.

Within a short period of time, he renounced the occult — even barging into a séance on one occasion and telling the participants to repent — and experienced a complete change of life. He became a Third Order Dominican and took the name "Br. Rosario." While on a business trip to the old destroyed city of Pompeii, he saw how spiritually poor the area was and decided to stay there and rebuild the city by spreading the rosary devotion.

He started orphanages, schools, and other works of mercy, and began construction on what would become the Pontifical Basilica of Our Lady of the Rosary of Pompeii, the most famous rosary shrine in the entire Catholic world.

Through the image of Our Lady of the Rosary that he placed inside the church, God brought about many healings, and it is the same image that is now associated with the 54-Day Rosary Novena to Our Lady of the Rosary of Pompeii (also known as the Irresistible Novena).

Bartolo Longo, the man who had once been an ordained priest of Satan, died in 1926 and was beatified by St. John Paul II in 1980.

Brings about Conversion

If the rosary is powerful enough to bring about the conversion of an ordained Satanic priest, it is powerful enough to bring about the conversion of any soul.

How does the rosary so effectively convert people, bringing them light and the fullness of truth?

Sister Lucia dos Santos provides a great answer to this question. She said:

> After the Holy Liturgy of the Eucharist, the prayer of the rosary is what better draws

to our spirit the mysteries of Faith, Hope, and Charity. She [the rosary] is the spiritual bread of souls.[2]

"The spiritual bread of souls." That is a powerful statement! Sister Lucia was not stating that the rosary is on the same level as our Lord in the Blessed Sacrament; she would never make such a claim. However, she draws our attention to something of fundamental importance regarding the power of the rosary: Namely, the rosary comes "after the Holy Liturgy of the Eucharist" in drawing us to the sacred mysteries of Jesus Christ.

According to St. Louis de Montfort, Our Lady herself spoke of the rosary as the greatest prayer after the Holy Sacrifice of the Mass. He wrote:

> One day Our Lady revealed to Blessed Alan that, after the Holy Sacrifice of the Mass, which is the most important as well as the living memorial of Our Blessed Lord's Passion, there could not possibly be a finer devotion or one of greater merit than that of the Holy Rosary, which is like a second memorial and representation of the Life and Passion of Our Lord Jesus Christ.[3]

In essence, the rosary flows from the greatest prayer, the Holy Sacrifice of the Mass. The rosary finds all its power in being united to the Holy Sacrifice of the Mass. This is what made a holy priest like the Dominican Fr. Marie Étienne Vayssière (1864–1940) state that his evening rosary was his "evening Communion." This saintly son of St. Dominic was so devoted to the rosary that he was said to "live the rosary" since he prayed it all throughout the day. He himself explained why he referred to his evening rosary as his "evening Communion":

> It [the rosary] is not merely a series of *Ave Marias* piously recited; it is Jesus living again in the soul through Mary's maternal action.[4]

The rosary brings souls to Jesus and Jesus to souls, all through Mary. The prayer of the rosary is essentially a mini catechism and New Testament on a string of beads. The truths contained in the sacred mysteries have the power to convert hearts and minds to the fullness of faith through infusing them with Divine Revelation. The meditative visualization (picturization) of the life-changing mysteries of Christianity is summed up in the mysteries of the rosary. To pray the rosary is to make a spiritual pilgrimage to the holy sites of our redemption. Praying the sacred mysteries of Jesus Christ leads us to conversion, Confession, and Communion.

Pope Pius XI put it this way:

> The rosary elevates minds to the truths re-
> vealed by God and shows us Heaven opened.
> The Virgin Mary herself has insistently
> recommended this manner of praying. All
> graces are conceded to us by God through
> the hands of Mary.[5]

The rosary has the power to bring about conversion because it leads us away from sin, directs us
to a life of virtue, and moves us to fully embrace the
teachings and Sacraments of the Catholic Church by
living a life of sanctifying grace. The rosary leads us to
Jesus Christ!

Is this not why the devotion most used by
mothers and grandmothers to get their children to
return to the faith has been the rosary? How many
people around the world attribute their return to the
faith to the rosaries prayed by their mother or grand-
mother! It makes perfect sense, then, why Mary,
our heavenly mother, in her approved apparitions
constantly urges us to pray the rosary as a means of
bringing about a deeper conversion in ourselves and
in all peoples.

A mother knows what works!

The Virgin Mary wants *all* people to pray the
rosary and undergo conversion. The rosary has the

power to bring *all* peoples to the fullness of truth found in Catholicism.

Here's a concrete example.

On October 7, 1901, two people who were then members of the Anglican Church, Fr. Paul Wattson (1863–1940) and Mother Lurana White (1870–1935), formed a movement called "The Rosary League of Our Lady of the Atonement." The purpose of the movement was to pray and work for the restoration of England to the Mother of God. Each member promised to pray at least three decades of the rosary a day for this intention. Incredibly, in 1909, Fr. Paul Wattson, Mother Lurana, and 15 others converted to Catholicism! It was the rosary that brought about their conversion to the fullness of the truth! (Father Paul Wattson is now a Servant of God and one day might even be declared a saint!)

Venerable Patrick Peyton — the priest responsible for gathering more people together to pray the rosary than any other person in the history of the Church — stated the following about how the rosary changes people:

> When you look at the rosary in your hand it appears very simple, that little string of beads, yet how far that short chain reaches, what a cosmos it encircles, how closely it

binds us to God and to Mary. You hold the power to change your lives![6]

Let's look at one dramatic example of the rosary's power to change a life.

The Beads of St. John Ogilvie

Have you ever heard of St. John Ogilvie?

Saint John was a very holy Jesuit priest who spread the Catholic faith during a time of great persecution. He was born in Scotland, educated in mainland Europe, and returned to his native country to preach the Gospel at a time when Catholics were being put to death.

In 1614, St. John was arrested in Glasgow and sent to jail in Paisley. He suffered terrible tortures during his imprisonment, including being kept awake for eight days and nights in an attempt to make him divulge the identities of other Catholics. Saint John was eventually convicted of high treason for refusing to accept the king's spiritual jurisdiction. He was sentenced to be hanged and disemboweled; he was only 36.

On the final day of his life, as he was being paraded through the streets of Glasgow, St. John clutched a rosary in his hand. His rosary had always been his lifeline to heaven; now he would hand that lifeline on to others. As he mounted the gallows in preparation for death, he threw his rosary to bystanders. The rosary struck the chest of a young nobleman named Baron John ab Eckersdorff. The baron was traveling through the town of Paisley on that day, and it was Eckersdorff's chest that was blessed with the touch of the martyr's beads. The event was so life changing that Eckersdorff later wrote it down in the following account:

> I was on my travels through England and Scotland — as is the custom of our nobility — being a mere stripling, and not having the faith. I happened to be in Glasgow the day Father Ogilvie was led forth to the gallows, and it is impossible for me to describe his lofty bearing in meeting death. His farewell to the Catholics was his casting into their midst from the scaffold, his rosary beads just before he met his fate. That rosary, thrown haphazard, struck me on the breast in such wise that I could have caught it in the palm of my hand; but there was such a rush and crush of the Catholics to get hold of it, that unless I wished to run the risk of being trodden down, I had to cast it from me. Religion was the last thing I was then thinking about: it was not in my mind at all;

yet from that moment I had no rest. Those rosary beads had left a wound in my soul; go where I would, I had no peace of mind. Conscience was disturbed, and the thought would haunt me: why did the martyr's rosary strike me, and not another? For years I asked myself this question — it followed me about everywhere. At last conscience won the day. I became a Catholic; I abandoned Calvinism; and this happy change I attribute to the martyr's beads, and to no other cause — those beads which, if I had them now, gold could not tempt me to part with; and if gold could purchase them, I should not spare it.[7]

WORDS OF WONDER

The rosary is the easiest way to honor God and the Blessed Virgin. It is the surest way to triumph over spiritual enemies, the most suitable way to progress in virtue and sanctity.[8]

Blessed James Alberione

The spirit of prayer and the practice of Christian life are best attained through the devotion of the rosary of Mary.[9]

Pope Leo XIII

Blessed Alan says that he has seen several people delivered from Satan's bondage after taking up the holy rosary, even though they had previously sold themselves to him in body and soul by renouncing their baptismal vows and their allegiance to Our Lord Jesus Christ.[10]

St. Louis de Montfort

WONDER 6

THE ROSARY IS THE FAVORED MARIAN DEVOTION OF POPES

Do not fail to put repeated emphasis on the recitation of the rosary, the prayer so pleasing to Our Lady and so often recommended by the Roman Pontiffs.[1]

St. Pope Paul VI

33 Miners in Chile

During the pontificate of Pope Benedict XVI, an event occurred in Chile that many consider miraculous. Many people are unaware that the rosary played a crucial role in this incredible event.

In August 2010, news reports around the world began to tell the story of the plight of 33 miners trapped 2,300 feet below the earth in a Chilean mine. As the daily reports continued, the entire world watched what seemed to be a completely hopeless situation. Every effort to make contact with the men failed. The miners were running out of supplies and going to die.

Incredibly — and to the surprise of the entire world — contact was made with the miners after 17 days! Engineers had been able to drill a small shaft down to precisely where the miners were imprisoned. Through this small shaft, food, water, and other supplies could be sent down to the trapped men. The ordeal was far from over, though. In order to save them, a much larger shaft had to be drilled, one that would allow them to be brought to the surface one by one. It would take a miracle for this to happen.

From St. Peter's in Rome, Pope Benedict XVI asked the entire world to pray for the miners. As a special sign of hope, the Pope personally blessed 33 rosaries and sent them to the miners so that they could pray the rosary and know that Jesus and Mary were with them. The blessed rosaries were sent down the small shaft to the men, and they began to pray them and wear them around their necks.

Miraculously, after having been trapped for 69 days, all 33 men survived and were rescued from the mine. One by one, they emerged from the depths of the earth and saw sunshine again. What was the date of their rescue? It was October 13, the anniversary of the Miracle of the Sun at Fatima!

Favored Marian Devotion of Popes

Did you know that within the first two weeks of the papacy of St. John Paul II, he informed the entire world that the rosary was his favorite prayer? He was elected to the papacy on October 16, 1978. He made this incredible statement about the rosary during his Angelus message on October 29, 1978.

Saint John Paul II was by no means the first pope to praise the rosary and extol its wonders. Over the last 800 years, a multitude of popes have spoken and written about the rosary, calling it the most praiseworthy form of devotion to Mary. They have not only exalted the rosary as *the* favored Marian devotion among popes, but have also declared it the crown of all devotions to the Mother of God.

From historical records, we know that the first pope to praise and promote the rosary was Pope Urban IV. He was pope during the century of St. Dominic, the founder of the rosary. After Pope Urban IV, every century has witnessed popes promoting the rosary. Some of these pontiffs truly stand out as champions of the rosary. Here are a few examples:

- 14th century
  - Pope John XXII grants indulgences to members of the Confraternity of the Rosary.

- 15th century
  - Pope Alexander VI establishes the "pious tradition" (the papal teaching that the rosary was founded by St. Dominic) .

- 16th century
  - Saint Pope Pius V saves Christianity and Western Civilization from Islamic takeover by means of the rosary. This Dominican pope also establishes Rosary Sunday and the Feast of Our Lady of Victory.
  - Pope Gregory XIII establishes the liturgical feast of Our Lady of the Rosary.

- 17th century
  - Pope Clement VIII restores the Church of St. Sixtus in Rome to the Dominicans. This is the church in which St. Dominic founded the Confraternity of the Rosary.

- 18th century
  - Pope Clement XI extends the liturgical feast of Our Lady of the Rosary to the entire Church.
  - Pope Benedict XIII, another holy Dominican pope, inserts the "pious tradition" into the Roman Breviary.

- 19th century
  - Pope Leo XIII writes 11 encyclicals on the rosary.

- 20th century
  - Saint Pope John XXIII and St. Pope Paul VI greatly promote the Family Rosary.
- 21st century
  - Saint Pope John Paul II offers the Church the Luminous Mysteries.

In their high praise for the rosary, popes have made it very clear that the rosary is for everyone, not just priests and nuns. Venerable Pope Pius XII mentioned this in one of his encyclicals:

> There are certain exercises of piety which the Church recommends very much to clergy and religious. It is our wish also that the faithful, as well, should take part in these practices. The chief of these are: meditation on spiritual things, diligent examination of conscience, enclosed retreats, visits to the Blessed Sacrament, and those special prayers in honor of the Blessed Virgin Mary, among which the rosary, as all know, has pride of place.[2]

According to the popes, the rosary truly has pride of place among all the prayers that honor Mary.

Perhaps the greatest statement ever made about the devotional primacy of the rosary came from St. Pope John XXIII when he noted the following:

As an exercise of Christian devotion among
the faithful of the Latin Rite who constitute
a notable portion of the Catholic family, the
rosary ranks after Holy Mass and the Breviary for ecclesiastics [priests], and for the
laity after participation in the sacraments. It
is a devout form of union with God and lifts
souls to a high supernatural plane.[3]

There really can be no greater praise given to
the rosary than for the Vicar of Christ to declare it
the highest exercise of Christian devotion possible
after the Sacraments and the Breviary (the Liturgy
of the Hours).

It was for this reason that several 20th-century
champions of the rosary — specifically Venerable
Patrick Peyton and the Servant of God Lucia Dos
Santos — boldly petitioned the pope to elevate the
rosary to the level of a liturgical prayer, similar to
the Mass and the Liturgy of the Hours! Though this
did not happen, the popes responded to the requests
of these two champions of the rosary by strongly
encouraging the Family Rosary.

Venerable Patrick Peyton knew firsthand how
powerful the Family Rosary was and dedicated his
entire priestly ministry to spreading this form of
devotion. He once said:

Because of the daily family rosary, my home was for me a cradle, a school, a university, a library, and most of all, a little church.[4]

Popes have long recognized the importance of the rosary in families and marriages. It's why popes hand out rosaries to newlyweds, at youth events, papal audiences, and other public celebrations. Saint John Paul II himself often made reference to the famous slogan popularized by Fr. Patrick Peyton — "The Family that Prays Together Stays Together." The Polish pope longed to see the restoration of the Family Rosary and greatly emphasized this in both a 1995 Angelus message and in his 2002 apostolic letter on the rosary:

> Daily recitation of the rosary in the family was once widespread. How worthwhile would such a practice be today! Mary's rosary removes the seeds of family breakup; it is the sure bond of communion and peace.[5]

> The family that prays together stays together. The holy rosary, by age-old tradition, has shown itself particularly effective as a prayer which brings the family together. Individual family members, in turning their eyes toward Jesus, also regain the ability to look

one another in the eye, to communicate, to show solidarity, to forgive one another and to see their covenant of love renewed in the Spirit of God.[6]

If the popes so highly praise the rosary, including the Family Rosary, individuals and families should at least be making efforts to pray it every day.

Pope Leo XIII
(The Pope of the Rosary)

There has never been a pope more dedicated to the promotion of the rosary than Pope Leo XIII.

The oldest pope in church history — he was 93 years old when he died — Pope Leo XIII held the office of Vicar of Christ for 25 years. During those 25 years, he wrote no fewer than 11 encyclicals on the rosary, as well as countless rosary-themed letters, exhortations, and messages. His 11 rosary encyclicals were written between the years 1883 and 1898. During those years, he wrote a rosary encyclical almost every year. No pope has ever written so many encyclicals on one single subject.

Listed below are his 11 rosary encyclicals in chronological order:

1883 — *Supremi Apostolatus Officio*
1884 — *Superiore Anno*
1887 — *Vi È Ben Noto*
1891 — *Octobri Mense*
1892 — *Magnae Dei Matris*
1893 — *Laetitiae Sanctae*
1894 — *Iucunda Semper Expectatione*
1895 — *Adiutricem Populi*
1896 — *Fidentem Piumque Animum*
1897 — *Augustissimae Virginis Mariae*
1898 — *Diuturni Temporis*

Nearly all of Pope Leo XIII's 11 rosary encyclicals were written in preparation for the month of October. He is largely responsible for turning October into a month completely dedicated to the rosary. In his youth, he had been very familiar with farm life and knew that October was the month for harvesting. That's why, during his papacy, he chose to promote the rosary in October to signify that the rosary is a way of reaping an abundant harvest of souls.

WORDS OF WONDER

When very frequently we receive newly married couples in audience and address paternal words to them, we give them rosaries, we recommend these to them earnestly, and we exhort them, citing our own example, not to let even one day pass without saying the rosary, no matter how burdened they may be with many cares and labors.[7]

Pope Pius XI

We now desire, as a continuation of the thought of our predecessors, to recommend strongly the recitation of the Family Rosary.[8]

St. Pope Paul VI

To return to the recitation of the Family Rosary means filling daily life with very different images, images of the mystery of salvation: the image of the Redeemer, the image of his most Blessed Mother. The family that recites the rosary together reproduces something of the atmosphere of the household of Nazareth: its members place Jesus at the center.[9]

St. John Paul II

WONDER 7

THE ROSARY IS ALWAYS PRAYED BY SAINTS

I wonder has there been any saint since the 13th century who did not use it [the rosary]?[1]

Servant of God Frank Duff

A Spanish Gypsy Takes a Bullet

> Blessed be the Lord my rock,
> who trains my hands for war,
> and my fingers for battle. (Ps 144:1)

Saints know they are in a battle against evil. In this battle, they never lay down their weapon. On a daily basis, the blessed beads of the rosary pass through their fingers as they meditate on the sacred mysteries of Jesus. Saints would rather die than be without the rosary.

Blessed Ceferino Giménez Malla is one of those heroes. A Spaniard, Bl. Ceferino was a gypsy who loved his rosary so much that he never let it fall from his hands, even to the point of giving his life. During the Spanish Civil War (1936–1939), he was arrested by the secular authorities for having given aid to a priest. The authorities instructed him to surrender his rosary or risk being shot. Blessed Ceferino adamantly refused to hand over his rosary, preferring to be shot and killed rather than give up his spiritual weapon. As a result, he took a bullet out of love for Jesus and Mary, and died with the rosary in his hand.

This heroic layman was beatified by St. John Paul II on May 4, 1997. In his homily for the beatification, the pope praised the example of holiness found in Blessed Ceferino:

> The gypsy Ceferino Giménez Malla, known as "El Pelé," died for the faith in which he had lived. His frequent participation at Mass, devotion to the Blessed Virgin with the recitation of the rosary, and his membership in various Catholic associations helped him to firmly love God and his neighbor. Thus even at the risk of his own life, he did not hesitate to defend a priest who was about to be arrested, and for doing so he was put in prison where he never ceased to pray and was later shot, as he clutched his rosary in his hands. Today, "El Pelé" intercedes for all

before our common Father, and the Church proposes him as a model to follow and a significant example of the universal vocation to holiness.[2]

Pope Benedict XVI also expressed a profound reverence for Blessed Ceferino in a papal address in 2011, even calling him a "martyr of the rosary":

His [Blessed Ceferino's] deep religious sense was expressed in his daily participation in Holy Mass and in the recitation of the rosary. The rosary beads themselves, which he always kept in his pocket, became the cause of his arrest and made Blessed Ceferino an authentic "martyr of the rosary," because he did not let anyone take the rosary from him, not even when he was at the point of death.[3]

Always Prayed by Saints

The rosary is the favored Marian devotion of the popes; it is also the favored Marian devotion of the saints. The rosary has played such a significant role in the lives of the saints that St. John Paul II highlighted that importance in his apostolic letter on the rosary in 2002. In that inspiring letter, he so emphasized the importance of the rosary in the spirituality of the saints that he arrived at the following conclusion:

> It would be impossible to name all the many saints who discovered in the rosary a genuine path to growth in holiness.[4]

Yes, it would be impossible. The Servant of God Frank Duff was absolutely correct when he wondered if there had been a single saint since the 13th century who had not prayed the rosary.

When the rosary was given to St. Dominic in the 13th century, no one on earth could have imagined the influence it would have in the lives of future heroes of the faith. Through the rosary, popes, priests, nuns, missionaries, laity, and even children would become virtuous and heroic promoters of the faith.

For example, at the time of the great missionary endeavors of the 16th century, Franciscans, Dominicans, Jesuits, and a whole host of other missionaries set out from Europe to the ends of the earth to evangelize the world. Traveling on the treacherous high seas to reach their destinations, the missionaries did not carry bulky liturgical items or dense theological tomes with them. They carried the rosary, the Bible on a set of beads, in their hands, and often around their waist. They evangelized entire continents by means of the rosary. It was in this same century that St. Francis de

Sales declared:

> If I did not have the obligation of the
> Divine Office [Breviary], I would say no
> other prayer than the rosary.[5]

That's a radical statement.

Saints are always radical.

There have been many saints who, like Bl. Ceferino Malla, have prayed the rosary during the last moments of their life as a further testimony to the power of this prayer. Saint Francisco Fernández de Capillas, a Spanish Dominican conducting missionary work in China, prayed the rosary in prison before being decapitated in 1648. In England, St. Oliver Plunkett devotedly prayed his rosary in prison before being executed in 1681. In the 17th century, the Ugandan martyrs of Africa — martyrs for purity and fidelity to the faith — did not let the rosary fall from their hands even as they were burned alive!

Modern times have also witnessed heroic examples of saints willing to die with the rosary in their hands. During the Mexican Cristero War in the 1920s, St. Miguel de la Mora, a member of the Knights of Columbus, became a martyr when he was shot while praying his rosary. During this same war, Blessed Miguel Pro was martyred for his faith by being shot by a firing squad. As he stood before the firing squad, he imitated Jesus by holding his arms outstretched as though on a cross. As he extended his arms, he held a crucifix in one hand and a rosary in the other. Before being shot, he cried out, "Viva Cristo Rey!"

And they were not alone. Many other faithful Mexican Catholics became martyrs around the same time. In fact, the atrocities against Catholics in Mexico in the early 20th century were so great that, in 1926, Pope Pius XI wrote an encyclical on the persecution of the Church in Mexico. The encyclical details many of the horrors that were being committed against Catholics. Pope Pius XI was so moved by the witness of the martyrs in Mexico that he made a point of drawing attention to the heroic example of the youth and their love of the rosary. He wrote:

> In narrating this, we can scarcely keep back our tears, for some of these young men and boys have gladly met death with the rosary in their hands and the name of Christ the King on their lips.[6]

During World War II, there were countless examples of heroic Catholics who were martyred because of their love of the rosary. Two Polish martyrs of the rosary were Blessed Władysław Demski and Blessed Józef Kowalski. Blessed Władysław was a diocesan priest taken prisoner by the Nazis in 1939 and eventually sent to the concentration camp in Sachsenhausen. While there, his rosary accidentally fell out of his pocket. A guard nearby saw it and threw it into the mud. The guard then mocked the priest and said that if he cared that much about it, he could find it in the mud and kiss it. Immediately Fr. Władysław knelt down, found the rosary in the mud, and kissed it while using it to make the Sign of the Cross on his lips. This action infuriated the guard and prompted the other guards to beat the priest to death.

Blessed Józef Kowalski's story is similar. He was a Salesian priest who had been arrested by the Gestapo in 1941 and sent to the Auschwitz concentration camp. One day during roll call, a guard knocked the rosary out of Fr. Józef's hand and commanded him to trample upon it. Father Józef refused, and was brutally tortured and drowned in a sewer shortly after. Saint John Paul II, who knew Bl. Józef Kowalski before the war, beatified both him and Fr. Demski in 1999 as two of the 108 Polish Martyrs of World War II.

Not all saints of the rosary are martyrs, though. Saint Anthony Mary Claret, a very holy priest from Spain who became a bishop in Cuba, required all the priests in his diocese to pray the rosary with their parishioners on Sundays and solemnities. He was so convinced of the power of the rosary that he wrote the following:

> Ever since the year 1208, during which the glorious St. Dominic taught people to pray it [the rosary] daily, there has not been a saint nor any person distinguished for learning and virtue, nor an observant religious community, nor a well-ordered seminary, which has not had the devotion to the rosary.[7]

All saints know the power of the rosary.

Saint Louis de Montfort, St. Pio of Pietrelcina, Blessed James Alberione, St. Marie Alphonsine Ghattas, and St. Josemaría Escrivá almost always had a rosary in their hand. Saint Josemaría Escrivá even wrote an entire book on the rosary in just one day!

Does all of this mean that the saints never struggled with praying the rosary? Of course not! The saints are human. They get distracted like the rest of us. It wasn't always easy for many of them to meditate and stay focused on the mysteries. The crucial difference of the saints, though, is that even in spite of struggles and difficulties in prayer, they never gave up.

The woman declared the greatest saint of modern times, St. Thérèse of Lisieux, struggled to pray the rosary. Her words are very comforting to those who do not find it easy to pray the rosary:

> I feel that I say the rosary so poorly! I make a concentrated effort to meditate on the mysteries of the rosary, but I am unable to focus my concentration. For a long time I was disconsolate about my lack of devotion, which astonished me since I so much loved the Blessed Virgin that it ought to have been easy for me to recite the prayers in her honor that so much pleased her. But now I am less sad, for I think that the Queen of heaven, who is also my Mother, ought to see my good intentions and that she is pleased with them.[8]

Saint Louis de Montfort himself fully acknowledged that it is quite normal to become distracted while praying the rosary. He wrote:

> You cannot possibly say your rosary without having a few involuntary distractions and it is hard to say even one Hail Mary without your imagination troubling you a little (for our imagination is, alas, never still).
>
> Being human, we easily become tired and slipshod — but the devil makes these difficulties worse when we are saying the rosary. Before we even begin he makes us

feel bored, distracted or exhausted — and when we have started praying he oppresses us from all sides.

Even if you have to fight distractions all through your whole rosary be sure to fight well, arms in hand: that is to say, do not stop saying your rosary even if it is hard to say and you have absolutely no sensible devotion. It is a terrible battle, I know, but one that is profitable to the faithful soul.[9]

Saint Teresa of Calcutta, who underwent years of spiritual dryness in prayer, never gave up praying the daily rosary. She knew the power of the rosary. Therefore, whether she had good feelings while praying the rosary or not, she nonetheless prayed it every day and always made sure that her religious sisters prayed it on a daily basis, especially as they ministered to the poorest of the poor:

When we walk the streets, in whatever part of the world, the sisters [Missionaries of Charity] carry in their hands the crown of the rosary. The Virgin is our strength and our protection.[10]

The rosary has been in the hands of saints for more than 800 years. If you want to be a saint, it should be in yours, too.

The Bilocations of Venerable
Mary of Ágreda

Venerable Mary of Ágreda is one of the greatest mystics of the 17th century. She was a Franciscan nun from Spain known for her heavenly visions and many mystical experiences. Her greatest work is a lengthy account of the life of the Virgin Mary, called the *Mystical City of God*. One of the most fascinating aspects of her life was her ability to mystically bilocate to the area of the American Southwest known today as New Mexico. These bilocations occurred between the years 1620–1623.

During these bilocations, she instructed the Jumano Indians in the truths and mysteries of Christianity. She informed them that Catholic priests would soon arrive in their area and bring the Sacraments to them. Incredibly, in 1629, Franciscan priests arrived in that exact region. When the Franciscan priests arrived, they were shocked to discover this tribe of Indians who were already familiar with the Catholic faith asking to be baptized and receive the Sacraments. The Indians even had rosaries in their hands!

Upon asking the Jumano Indians how they had acquired their knowledge of Catholicism and obtained rosaries, the Franciscans were informed by the tribe that, for several years, a "Lady in Blue" had visited them, instructed them, and given them rosaries. The missionaries initially thought that the Indians had been blessed with apparitions of the Virgin Mary. However, when the Franciscans showed the Indians an image of the Virgin Mary, the tribe said it was not Our Lady who had visited them, but another woman dressed in blue. After sharing this information with their superiors back in Spain, the friars were able to ascertain and verify that the woman who had been appearing in the American Southwest was none other than the famed Spanish mystic Mary of Ágreda! During an investigation into these remarkable events, Mary of Ágreda confirmed her bilocations to the Jumano tribe. She also noted that during her frequent bilocations, she would take piles of rosaries from her convent and distribute them to the Indians.

WORDS OF WONDER

May the rosary never fall from your hands![11]

St. Pope John XXIII

In moments when fever, agony, and pain make it hard to pray, the suggestion of prayer that comes from merely holding the rosary — or better still, from caressing the Crucifix at the end of it — is tremendous.[12]

Venerable Fulton J. Sheen

Confidently take up the rosary once again. Rediscover the rosary in light of Scripture, in harmony with the liturgy, and in the context of your daily lives. May this appeal of mine not go unheard![13]

St. John Paul II

WONDER 8

THE ROSARY CHANGES
HISTORY AND BRINGS PEACE

*What fruits the world and the Church
owe to the rosary![1]*

Servant of God Joseph Kentenich

Routing a Communist-Leaning
President in Brazil

One of the most inspiring rosary victories of
the 20th century took place in Brazil in 1964.
When the country was being governed by the com-
munist-leaning President João Goulart, large groups
of people turned to the rosary and rose up in rebellion against their oppressive leaders. Rosary groups
formed and were able to break up communist rallies
by marching in the streets, loudly praying the rosary.

One famous event occurred in the city of
Belo Horizonte, where a communist rally was taking

place under the direction of President Goulart. The president had already appointed many communists to high positions in the government and was now rallying support in Belo Horizonte for a communist revolution in Brazil. The archbishop of Rio de Janeiro, Cardinal de Barros Camara, spoke against the president by going on national radio to ask the people of Brazil to live the message of Fatima as a means of overcoming the communist threat. President Goulart was so enraged by the archbishop's messages that he insulted the people of Brazil in a public speech and ridiculed the rosary, saying that it was his communist ideas that would reform and save Brazil, not the rosaries of simple women. These words greatly upset the Brazilian people, and they decided to confront the communists during the rally in Belo Horizonte.

The rally in Belo Horizonte was led by Goulart's brother-in-law, Leonel Brizola, and it was intended to be one of the largest communist rallies in the country. As it was taking place, more than 20,000 women marched into the streets with rosaries in their hands to engage in spiritual battle! They marched right into the midst of the communist rally and prayed the rosary so loudly that it shut the rally down. On March 19, only six days after the women broke up the communist rally, more than 600,000 people marched through the streets of São Paolo praying the rosary in the famous "March of the Family with God toward Freedom." Initially this march was called the "March to Make Amends to the Rosary," since President Goulart had insulted the rosary in his public speech. However, the name was changed so that non-Catholics would participate as well. Many non-Catholics did attend the march and prayed the rosary with the Catholics as they marched in defiance against the president's communist vision. Goulart was so intimidated by the rosary army that within two weeks he had fled the country! In thanksgiving for the rosary victory, the people of Brazil organized another march in gratitude to Our Lady and her rosary. It was held on April 2, 1964, one day after President Goulart fled the country. This march was called the "March of Thanksgiving to God." More than a million people marched through the streets of Rio de Janeiro, celebrating their freedom from the threat of communism.

Changes History and Brings Peace

For more than 800 years, the rosary has been a game-changer in both civil and religious affairs.

How is this possible?

The answer is simple: Prayer changes things.

Prayer changes people, situations, and even history itself.

The prayer of the rosary, in particular, is grounded in the transforming power of God's holy Word. Remember: God's Word does not return to him void. When he sends out his Word, it always bears fruit. The rosary is composed of the Word of God. The rosary is the ultimate game-changer!

The ability of the rosary to change history and bring about peace is why Pope Leo XIII strongly emphasized the positive effects of the rosary on society. He stressed this in all of the 11 encyclicals on the rosary that he wrote. He, and so many other popes, understood the rosary to be a supernatural means of establishing social peace and the preservation of Christian virtues and culture. One only has to remember the battles that took place at Muret, Malta, Lepanto, and Vienna (Lepanto and Vienna will be covered in Wonder 9) to remember that it was the rosary that restored peace and saved towns, countries, and civilization itself.

Saint Anthony Mary Claret emphasized the personal and societal effects of the rosary in these words:

> The devotion of the most holy rosary is powerful enough to transmit all graces and, as we are aware from experience, it has proven to be a remedy during times of war, plagues, hunger and other calamities; in addition, those who have been troubled in body or soul, if they had recourse to the rosary, always received consolation.[2]

Saint Anthony is absolutely correct. The rosary not only changes history, but also brings consolation and peace to human hearts. The rosary is a peacemaker.

The rosary's power to bring about peace is one of the reasons why this devotion is most often a major part of approved Marian apparitions. Mary, our spiritual mother, wants her children to have peace. In this regard, the Servant of God Frank Duff, founder of the Legion of Mary, wrote the following:

> The rosary was established about the year 1200 and it took from the first minute. It was proposed to people and they were encouraged to use it. It proved itself to have an affinity for the people. Ever since, it has been intertwined with Catholic life. It has been prominent in devotional literature; an element in the lives of the holy ones of the Church; the subject of the teachings of the

Popes and the Doctors. The rosary has been carried by Our Lady in many of the accepted apparitions. It has entered into many of the recorded miraculous events, some of which have saved the world. It is believed to have been responsible for innumerable favors.[3]

Here's proof of what Frank Duff is alluding to.

At Lourdes, Fatima, Beauraing, and Banneux, Mary carried the rosary on her person. At Fatima, Mary referred to herself as "The Lady of the Rosary." At many other approved apparitions, too, the rosary has been at the heart of the messages given by Our Lady: Akita, Japan; Cuapa, Nicaragua; Kibeho, Rwanda (Africa); and San Nicolas, Argentina. When a person studies the approved Marian apparitions, there can be no doubt that the most common themes that Mary emphasizes are prayer, conversion, penance, and the rosary.

Our spiritual mother knows that prayerful meditation on the sacred mysteries of Jesus Christ moves hearts toward her Son. In response to such prayer, Jesus gives unimaginable graces to the world. These graces bring peace.

The rosary is divine therapy for the wounded mind, heart, and soul.

The rosary is a remedy for the ills of society!

When prayed against the political ideologies of leaders whose agendas are not pleasing to God, the rosary changes history and brings peace!

When prayed against the ancient serpent who seeks to destroy marriages (even striving to have marriage redefined), the rosary changes history and brings peace!

When prayed against the filthy images of pornography, the slavery of drug addiction, the lure of the occult, and the worship of self, the rosary changes history and bring peace!

The rosary is an antidote that gets the poison of the world out of our hearts.

The Servant of God Joseph Kentenich understood this very well. At the beginning of the 20th century, he understood there was a great need for the Church to address the anthropological crises (mistaken views on human nature and our place in the world) of our times. To do this, he initiated a movement that would reeducate people in Christian truths and virtues: the Schoenstatt movement. An extremely holy priest, Fr. Kentenich strongly recommended to the members of his movement to pray the rosary because the rosary has the power to transform the world and overcome heresies (false teachings). He said:

> The great remedy of modern times which will influence the events of the world more than all diplomatic endeavors and which has a greater effect on public life than all organizational ones, is the rosary.[4]

Father Kentenich is absolutely correct. It is not the wisdom of men that will heal our world. Man-made peace treaties are *always* temporary; such accords only offer a bandaid to a spiritual problem. What offers true and lasting peace are the saving mysteries of Jesus Christ. Jesus himself tells us in the Gospel of John, "Peace I leave with you; my peace I give to you. Not as the world gives do I give it to you" (Jn 14:27).

Sister Lucia Dos Santos, who spoke to Our Lady face-to-face, gives us this lesson on the ability of the rosary to alter any situation and bring peace:

> The Most Holy Virgin, in these last times in which we live, has given a new efficacy to the recitation of the rosary to such an extent that there is no problem, no matter how difficult it is, whether temporal or above all spiritual, in the personal life of each one of us, of our families ... that cannot be solved by the rosary. There is no problem, I tell you, no matter how difficult it is, that we cannot resolve by the prayer of the holy rosary.[5]

The Rosary Crusades of Venerable Patrick Peyton

In the mid-to-late 20th century, the Irish-born Fr. Patrick Peyton carried out an extremely popular worldwide rosary apostolate known as the Family Rosary Crusade. His crusades brought about much good for society and the family.

In the early 1940s, Fr. Peyton began his promotion of the rosary by writing to bishops in the United States and encouraging them to promote the Family Rosary. In 1947, Fr. Peyton officially launched his rosary crusades on a national and international scale. On fire with a desire to bring the rosary to the entire world, Fr. Peyton traveled to more than 40 countries and was able to gather more than 28 million people to pray the rosary! Remarkably, during the 1950s, he was even able to gather some of the leading actors in Hollywood to publicly pray the rosary on the radio and national television.

When the turbulent era of the 1960s began, Fr. Peyton was one of the few figures who continued to be able to draw large groups of people to pray the rosary. In San Francisco in 1961, he was able to bring together more than a half-million people for a rosary gathering for the archdiocese.

He took his rosary crusade to other countries, as well. Father Peyton gathered millions of people together in rosary rallies in places such as Colombia, Brazil, and the Philippines. His rosary apostolate flourished in those countries and was often credited with bringing about peace and positive change.

Father Peyton coined the catchy slogans, "The family that prays together stays together," and "A world at prayer is a world at peace." To this day, Fr. Peyton's efforts remain unparalleled.

WORDS OF WONDER

Those who pray the rosary do more for the benefit of the whole human race than all the orators and deputies, more than all the organizers, secretaries, and writers, more than all the capitalists even if they would make their entire wealth available to the Church.[6]

Servant of God Joseph Kentenich

The rosary of Mary is the great lever, it is the anchor of salvation for society and for individuals. Lepanto and Vienna are names associated with the rosary. The victories over the Albigensians, over French philosophism, over liberalism and modernism find their explanation in the rosary.[7]

Blessed James Alberione

No normal mind yet has been overcome by worries or fears who was faithful to the rosary. You will be surprised how you can climb out of your worries, bead by bead, up to the very throne of the Heart of Love itself.[8]

Venerable Fulton J. Sheen

WONDER 9

THE ROSARY OVERCOMES RADICAL ISLAM

*She [Mary] will renew the
wonders of Lepanto!*[1]

Pope Leo XIII

A Bishop in Nigeria, Boko Haram, and a Sword

In April 2014, Boko Haram kidnapped more than 200 young girls from a school in Nigeria, Africa. Boko Haram is the notorious radical Muslim group that violently slaughters non-Muslims by such means as decapitation or burning people alive.

In December 2014, Jesus appeared to a Catholic bishop in Nigeria and instructed him that the rosary was the weapon that would overcome Boko Haram. Bishop Oliver Dashe Doeme of the diocese of Maiduguri, Nigeria, claims that one evening, while he was praying his rosary, Jesus appeared to him holding a sword. During the vision, Jesus extended the sword toward the bishop. When the bishop went to take the sword from Jesus, it miraculously transformed into a rosary! Once the bishop had the rosary-sword in his hands, Jesus looked at him and said three times, "Boko Haram is gone! Boko Haram is gone! Boko Haram is gone!"

After the bishop of Maiduguri had his vision, he began to promote the rosary in his diocese in Nigeria. In many of his interviews, he repeats his vision and informs his listeners of his interpretation of the vision in the following words: "As soon as I received the sword, it turned into a rosary. I didn't need any prophet to give me the explanation. It was clear that with the rosary we would be able to expel Boko Haram."[2] On October 13, 2016, dozens of kidnapped girls were suddenly released by Boko Haram from captivity. In May 2017, another 83 girls were released. Then, on July 3, 2017, 700 members of Boko Haram surrendered their weapons and turned themselves in to Nigerian authorities.

Overcomes Radical Islam

The religion of Islam came into existence in the seventh century. From its beginning, Islam has had various groups within it that have sought to conquer and eradicate Christianity. As a result, numerous battles have taken place between Christianity and Islam over the past 1,300 years. There is one battle, however, that stands out from all the rest: the Battle of Lepanto. It was a decisive battle, one that saved Christianity and Western Civilization from Islamic takeover.

The Servant of God Joseph Kentenich offers a brief synopsis of the Battle of Lepanto:

> In the 16th century, the archenemy [the Muslim Turks] threatened all the port cities of the Mediterranean with its terrible fleet. Pius V brought together an armada in union with Spain, Venice, and the Knights of Malta, with Don Juan as admiral. Pius himself, a second Moses, set himself at the head of a storm of prayer. At his word, the rosary was prayed by all Christianity in order to secure Mary's favor in the decisive battle upon which the fate of Italy and all Europe depended.[3]

A holy pope, a pious admiral, and a lot of people praying the rosary were all it took to overcome Muslim extremists.

Here's a condensed version of the story of the Battle of Lepanto in all its wonder.

Saint Pope Pius V, a Dominican pope, knew that if Europe were to be saved from the threat of radical Islam, it would only come about through the intercession of the Virgin Mary. It was his initiative to organize a Christian militia and ask all of Christendom to pray the rosary for victory against the Muslim threat. In preparation for the confrontation, Pope Pius V handpicked Don Juan of Austria to be commander of the Christian fleet. (See the cover for a depiction of Don Juan.)

Acclaimed by G.K. Chesterton as the last knight of Europe, Don Juan knew that he was about to engage in a holy war with Islam. Prior to sailing off to war, he gave orders that all blasphemy was forbidden on his ships and required that all of his men fast for three days. He forbade women from entering his vessels, lest any of his men fall into the sin of lust and mar their souls before battle. He ensured that his vessels would have priests available to hear Confessions and grant absolution. He also distributed a rosary to every man in his armada. Then, on the eve of battle, leading by example, he required that all of his men take the spiritual sword of the rosary into their hands and pray it — and they did.

Likewise, on the evening of October 6, 1571, the day before the decisive battle, St. Pope Pius V himself led the rosary at the Dominican convent of Santa Maria Sopra Minerva in Rome. With tears in his eyes and a rosary in his hand, he entrusted the Christian cause to the Queen of Heaven.

On the morning of October 7, 1571, the Christian fleet set sail in search of the Muslim fleet to meet them head on. Don Juan and his men had no idea that they were sailing toward an advanced and highly trained Muslim fleet of more than 300 vessels and 100,000 men. Though the Christian fleet had close to 285 vessels, they only had 70,000 men, many of whom were unskilled in naval combat. The two forces caught sight of each other for the first time in the large bay just south of the town of Lepanto (now Nafpaktos), Greece. Once they saw each other, they formed their battle lines. The battle was on. It was the cross versus the crescent.

The battle lasted for five bloody hours. At one point, Don Juan steered his vessel toward the vessel from which Ali Pasha commanded the Islamic forces. Before the two flagships collided and their crews could engage in hand-to-hand combat, Don Juan, filled with the Spirit of God, danced with abandon on the deck of his ship. This act enraged Ali Pasha, but he was unable to take his revenge because a musket ball to the forehead immediately killed him. One of the armed prisoners who had been freed from the Muslim ship cut off what was left of Ali Pasha's head and hoisted it on a pike. The banner of Allah was taken down and ripped apart, and the banner of St. Pope Pius V was raised in its place.

The battle was a complete success for the Catholic forces. The Turkish fleet lost more than 30,000 men. Thirty-four Muslim admirals and 120 galley captains were among the dead. The Muslim fleet also lost the majority of its vessels. The Christian fleet was able to set free nearly 15,000 Christian galley slaves who had been aboard the Muslim vessels. It was a complete and total victory for Christianity.

What is less well known about the Battle of Lepanto is that Our Lady of Guadalupe was there. In the battle formation of the Christian fleet, a decorated admiral named Giovanni Andrea Doria was in charge of the right wing of the fleet. Aboard his galley ship, he carried a most precious gift, given to him by King Philip of Spain: a replica of the image of Our Lady of Guadalupe that had been touched to the original!

As history attests, after the apparitions of Our Lady of Guadalupe occurred in Mexico in 1531, Archbishop Montufar of Mexico City had five copies of the miraculous image made. Each was touched to the original image. One of these images was given to the king of Spain in 1570. King Philip, in turn, gave his copy to Admiral Doria, who brought the image with him on his ship to the Battle of Lepanto. Our Lady of Guadalupe, La Conquistadora, had conquered the false gods of the Aztecs in Mexico; she returned to Europe to be present at the decisive Battle of Lepanto and defeat the Islamic threat.

Also present at the Battle of Lepanto was Miguel Cervantes, the famed author of Spain's greatest novel, *Don Quixote*. One of the many valiant men who had come to the defense of Christianity, Cervantes was severely wounded at the Battle of Lepanto, and wrote the following about the battle that saved the west:

> Ages gone by have seen nothing like unto the Battle of Lepanto, nor has our age witnessed anything to compare with it, and in all probability ages to come will never record a more beautiful or glorious triumph for the Church.[4]

The Battle of Lepanto did indeed save Christianity from Islamic takeover. Yet, as glorious as the

Battle of Lepanto was for Christianity, there are signs today that an even more glorious triumph over Islam will occur in the future.

Venerable Fulton J. Sheen believed that this future victory would once again come about through the intercession of the Virgin Mary. He states:

> At the present time, the hatred of the Muslim countries against the West is becoming a hatred against Christianity itself. Although the statesmen have not yet taken it into account, there is still grave danger that the temporal power of Islam may return and, with it, the menace that it may shake off a West that has ceased to be Christian and affirm itself as a great anti-Christian world power. Muslim writers say, "When the locust swarms darken vast countries, they bear on their wings these Arabic words: 'We are God's host, each of us has ninety-nine eggs, and if we had a hundred, we should lay waste the world with all that is in it.'" The problem is: How shall we prevent the hatching of the hundredth egg? It is our firm belief that the fears some entertain concerning the Muslims are not to be realized, but that Islam, instead, will eventually be converted to Christianity — and in a way that even some of our missionaries never suspect. It is

our belief that this will happen not through the direct teaching of Christianity but through a summoning of the Muslims to a veneration of the Mother of God.[5]

Fulton Sheen is right. The "hatching of the hundredth egg" of Islam is only going to be prevented by means of veneration of the Mother of God. History has shown that dialogue with Islam is not going to bring Muslims to Jesus Christ. Something much more powerful than dialogue is needed.

In some of his other writings, Fulton Sheen suggests that Mary's apparitions in Fatima, Portugal, will play a major role in bringing about the conversion of Muslims to Catholicism. The town of Fatima, after all, is named after one of the daughters of Mohammed. Also, the mother of Jesus is the only woman mentioned by name in the Koran — not even Mohammed's own mother is named. The Mother of Jesus can — and will — lead the followers of Mohammed to Jesus Christ. Many Muslims already pray on a string of beads that looks very similar to the rosary; several mysteries of the rosary are even present in the Koran (the Annunciation, Visitation, and Nativity). If Muslims come to Jesus Christ and Catholicism, it will be through Mary. The exchange of Muslim prayer beads for the rosary will be an easy one.

There must be a reason why God has allowed Islam to flourish and spread all over the globe. Is God planning something absolutely wonderful for our times, an event that would lead an entire religion (Islam) to convert to Catholicism? If the Holy Trinity were to work a miracle similar to that which occurred in Mexico with Our Lady of Guadalupe in the 16th century, we would undoubtedly witness the conversion of millions of Muslims to the fullness of the truth in Catholicism.

Will this happen? We don't know.

But we can speculate how it might.

Dare we hope that the Holy Trinity will send the Mother of God to Mecca to stand atop the Kaaba? If such an event were to occur, I guarantee she will be holding the Christ Child in one hand and a rosary in the other.

May Our Lady of the Rosary bring the Muslims to Jesus Christ and Catholicism!

The Battle of Vienna

In the 17th century, the Ottoman Turks (Muslims) were once again on a rampage in Eastern Europe, besieging town after town in their efforts to spread Islam. In 1683, they made their way toward the key city of Vienna.

Muslims had tried to take the city before and failed, but now, with an army of more than 150,000 soldiers (some of whom were Protestant), they sought to conquer Vienna in the name of Allah. In imitation of what St. Pope Pius V had done in the previous century, Blessed Pope Innocent XI formed a Holy League and entrusted the defense of Vienna to the Blessed Virgin Mary. His Holy League was comprised of armies from Poland, Germany, and France. The military commander of the army was King Jan Sobieski of Poland.

Although the city of Vienna was already under siege by the Muslims when Jan Sobieski set out from Warsaw with his 40,000 troops on the 435-mile march to the battlefront, Sobieski's forces marched with determination and resolve, entrusting their mission to Jesus and Mary. In fact, before they began their journey, Jan Sobieski made a detour and brought his entire army before the famous image of Our Lady of Czestochowa, entrusting their cause to the Mother of God.

The long march of the army turned into a tremendous rosary procession through fields and towns across Europe. Men prayed the rosary every day, sometimes individually and other times in large groups. By the time Sobieski's rosary army finally arrived at Vienna, the Muslims had been attacking the city for two months. The Christian forces inside the city were in desperate need of assistance. The Muslims had caused major damage to the city and were now very close to breaching the city walls.

On the morning of September 12, 1683 (the Feast of the Holy Name of Mary), Jan Sobieski attended Mass, entrusted his army to the hands of the Virgin Mary, and began his assault against the Muslims. As Sobieski's soldiers ran with abandon down the hill toward the Muslim army, they shouted aloud, "Jesus and Mary, save us!" And Jesus and Mary did save them, as well as the city of Vienna. The Muslims were defeated in a matter of hours. Our Lady of the Rosary had been victorious again!

After the battle, King Jan Sobieski related the events of the victory to Pope Innocent XI, describing to the pontiff exactly what had happened that day. He said, "I came, I saw, God conquered!"[6] Upon his return to Poland, Jan Sobieski went immediately to the shrine of Our Lady of Czestochowa on a pilgrimage of thanksgiving and laid the banners captured from the defeated Muslim army before the miraculous image.

WORDS OF WONDER

It is said that the Pontiff [St. Pius V] knew by Divine Revelation of the victory of Lepanto achieved at that very moment when through the Catholic world the pious sodalities of the holy rosary implored the aid of Mary in that formula initiated by the Founder of the Friar Preachers and diffused far and wide by his followers.[7]

Pope Benedict XV

Missionaries in the future will, more and more, see that their apostolate among the Muslims will be successful in the measure that they preach Our Lady of Fatima. Mary is the advent of Christ, bringing Christ to the people before Christ himself is born. In any apologetic endeavor, it is always best to start with that which people already accept. Because the Muslims have a devotion to Mary, our missionaries should be satisfied merely to expand and to develop that devotion, with the full realization that Our Blessed Lady will carry the Muslims the rest of the way to her Divine Son.[8]

Venerable Fulton J. Sheen

In the present international situation, I appeal to all — individuals, families, and communities — to pray the rosary for peace, even daily, so that the world will be preserved from the dreadful scourge of terrorism.[9]

St. John Paul II

WONDER 10

THE ROSARY IS AN
INDULGENCED PRAYER

*It is not without reason that the Supreme
Pontiffs have strongly recommended
this practice [the rosary], enriching it
with indulgences.*[1]

Blessed James Alberione

A Tiny, Eerie Museum in Rome

Many people who visit Rome, Italy, are unaware that near St. Peter's Basilica and the Vatican is a tiny museum dedicated to the Holy Souls in Purgatory. The Piccolo Museo del Purgatorio (Little Museum of Purgatory) is located inside the Chiesa del Sacro Cuore del Suffragio (Church of the Sacred Heart of Suffrage) and has a fascinating history, as well as an eerie collection of items on display.

In 1897, a chapel under the patronage of Our Lady of the Rosary, part of the property of a religious order in Rome dedicated to the Sacred Heart of Jesus, caught on fire. After the fire, members of the religious order noticed an image of a suffering face charred on one of the remaining walls. The priests and brothers immediately understood it as a sign from a soul in purgatory that it was in need of prayer. One member in particular, Fr. Victor Jouet, was quite moved by the sign and made it his mission to bring a greater awareness to the world of the need to pray for the souls in purgatory. He received permission from his superior to search all over Europe for extraordinary items similar to the suffering face on the charred church wall. In 1917, when the religious order opened a new church in Rome dedicated to the Sacred Heart of Jesus, they also dedicated a tiny museum within the church to the souls in purgatory, a museum that contained all the items collected by Fr. Jouet.

What are these items? The majority of the collection consists of singed handprints on clothing, books, or wood. Each one has a story behind it, a story that involves a soul in purgatory appearing to the living and asking for help finding relief from their suffering and longing for God; the singe mark left behind by the soul is a verification of the truth of the message.

One of these items dates from 1815. It is a page from the popular devotional book *The Imitation of Christ*. On the page is a singed handprint. The singed handprint appeared on the book when a woman who had died in 1785 appeared to her daughter-in-law and said that she was in purgatory and needed prayers. Initially, the daughter-in-law was skeptical and asked for a sign. At that very moment, there appeared on the pages of *The Imitation of Christ*, the book that the daughter-in-law was reading, the singed handprint of her mother-in-law!

All of the items in the museum bear witness to the reality that we need to pray for the souls in purgatory, especially by means of the Holy Mass and the holy rosary.

An Indulgenced Prayer

Did you know that after the Holy Mass, the rosary is one of the best ways to help the souls in purgatory? That's because the holy rosary is one of the most heavily indulgenced prayers of the Church.

Sadly, many people no longer understand the importance of indulgences. Some people have even been taught that indulgences are something the Catholic Church made up and have no basis in reality. Nothing could be further from the truth. Indulgences are in perfect harmony with reason and the order of justice as revealed by God.

Allow me to explain by using an analogy.

Let's say one day you are playing baseball in your backyard. It's your turn to bat. You swing and hit the ball so hard that it goes out of your yard and through the neighbor's window, shattering it into a thousand pieces. Not good. In all likelihood, however, when you explain to your neighbor what happened, he will understand and forgive you. Your neighbor is not going to be happy about the broken window, but he will most likely extend forgiveness. Does that forgiveness mean you are completely off the hook? No, it doesn't. The neighbor has forgiven you for breaking the window, but he is still going to ask you to repair the damage done when you broke his window. Repairing his window is a matter of justice. You owe him a new window.

Fulfilling the order of justice is also how the saving mission of Jesus Christ works. Through the Life, Death, and Resurrection of our Savior, we are forgiven of our sins, forgiven for the stuff we broke. That forgiveness is given to us through the Catholic

Church, the Mystical Body of Christ, which extends to us the absolute certainty of God's forgiveness through the Sacrament of Reconciliation (Confession). Yet God is just, and he knows that our sins have effects that remain — the stuff we broke. He also knows we are finite and can never fully restore the damage we have caused by our sins. Thus, in addition to forgiving our sins, he also provides a treasure trove of blessings that the Church can dispense to us so that we can make amends for the wrong we have done. He *indulges* us with his mercy. This means we receive God's forgiveness and fulfill the demands of justice by means of the grace he has given us.

God knows that we have to "fix what we have broken." This is why we have indulgences.

So what is an indulgence? The *Catechism of the Catholic Church* defines an indulgence in this way:

> An indulgence is a remission before God of the temporal punishment due to sins whose guilt has already been forgiven, which the faithful Christian who is duly disposed gains under certain prescribed conditions through the action of the Church which, as the minister of redemption, dispenses and applies with authority the treasury of the satisfactions of Christ and the saints.

An indulgence is partial or plenary according
as it removes either part or all of the temporal
punishment due to sin. The faithful can gain
indulgences for themselves or apply them to
the dead.[2]

Whoa! This means that the rosary is not only
powerful enough to help the living avoid purgatory,
but also powerful enough to help the dead who are
already in purgatory get out!

Through the rosary, we have the ability to gain
partial indulgences (the kind of indulgence that takes
care of some of the temporal punishment due to sin
— that is, time in purgatory) and plenary indulgences
(the kind of indulgence that takes care of all the temporal punishment due to sin).

How important is it for people to understand
indulgences? It's very important.

Once a person dies, they no longer have time
to make satisfaction for their sins, fix the stuff they
broke, and fulfill the order of justice. If they have
been blessed to avoid hell and go to purgatory, they
will be there until they fulfill the order of justice
through purification, or their time will be quickened
through the indulgences that are gained for them
from members of the Church Militant, those of us
still on earth. The souls in purgatory won't be in

purgatory forever, but we can greatly help them to get to the Beatific Vision sooner if we gain indulgences for them. Wouldn't you want someone to do that for you?

Today, many people are under the impression that when they die they go straight to heaven. The reality is that unless a person has lived a very holy life here on earth (by prayer, penance, and good works), they are going to need to make amends for the damage they have done by their sins. Let me give you a few statistics that may surprise you:

- Every hour on this planet, more than 6,000 people die

- Every day on this planet, more than 150,000 people die

- Every year on this planet, more than 55 million people die

Did you know that?

The reality is that most of these people are not prepared for death. Hopefully, they have cried out to God and received his mercy. Yet, when a person dies, their time is up. This means that the majority of people who die are not free of the temporal punishment due to sin. But we can help them!

This is why the rosary has traditionally been prayed at funerals: in order to gain indulgences for the deceased so that their purification will be quickened. Praying the rosary at a funeral is not primarily for the consolation of the family and friends of the deceased, but for the indulgences gained for the deceased person.

In modern times, people are too quick to canonize their relatives and friends at funerals. The greatest thing that can be done for a deceased friend or relative (or a complete stranger) is to gain an indulgence for them. If poor Uncle Joe wants anything from you at his funeral, it would be an indulgence gained by praying the rosary!

In *The Secret of the Rosary,* St. Louis de Montfort notes how St. Dominic stressed the indulgenced aspect of the rosary when he gave penances during Confession:

> Saint Dominic was so convinced of the efficacy of the holy rosary and of its great value that, when he heard confessions, he hardly ever gave any other penance. Saint Dominic was a great saint and other confessors should be sure to walk in his footsteps by asking their penitents to say the rosary together with meditation on the sacred mysteries, rather than giving them other penances which are less meritorious and

less pleasing to God, less likely to help them advance in virtue and not as efficacious as the rosary for helping them avoid falling into sin. Moreover, while saying the rosary, people gain countless indulgences which are not attached to many other devotions.[3]

Blessed Alan de la Roche, the great restorer of the rosary, also promoted the indulgences attached to the rosary, especially for the souls in purgatory. We learn the following from St. Alphonsus Liguori, a Doctor of the Church:

> Blessed Alan writes that many of the [Dominican] brethren had appeared to them while reciting the rosary, and had declared that next to the Holy Sacrifice of the Mass there was no more powerful means than the rosary to help the suffering souls [in purgatory]. Numerous souls were released daily who otherwise would have been obliged to remain in purgatory for years.[4]

According to St. Louis de Montfort, Our Lady herself revealed these truths to Blessed Alan de la Roche:

> Our Lady said to Blessed Alan: "I want you to know that, although there are numerous indulgences already attached to the recitation of my rosary, I shall add many more to

every fifty Hail Marys (each group of five decades) for those who say them devoutly, on their knees — being, of course, free from mortal sin. And whosoever shall persevere in the devotion of the holy rosary, saying these prayers and meditations, shall be rewarded for it; I shall obtain for him full remission of the penalty and of the guilt of all his sins at the end of his life. Do not be unbelieving, as though this is impossible. It is easy for me to do because I am the Mother of the King of heaven, and he calls me full of grace. And, being full of grace, I am able to dispense grace freely to my dear children."[5]

Throughout the centuries, saints like St. Juan Macias (1585–1645) and St. Stanislaus Papczynski (1631–1701) exhibited great zeal in praying for the souls in purgatory and gaining indulgences for them. Saint Juan Macias was a Dominican who served in South America, and St. Stanislaus Papczynski was a Polish priest and mystic who founded the first men's religious community in the Church dedicated to the Immaculate Conception — the Marian Fathers of the Immaculate Conception. The Marian Fathers continue to carry out the special charism of their Founder by praying for the souls in Purgatory every day. The rosary is part of the daily prayers of the Marians Fathers.

Here are a few statements from other saints about praying the rosary for the souls in purgatory:

> The rosary, which the Church so highly recommends, is not only the font of many graces for the living, but also a most powerful means of aiding the dead.[6]

> Blessed James Alberione

> If we want to help the souls in purgatory then we should say the rosary for them because the rosary gives them great relief.[7]

> St. Alphonsus Liguori

> The most holy rosary is an abundant mine through which Christians, praying and meditating with attention and devotion, become enriched with great merits.[8]

> St. Anthony Mary Claret

"How do you gain an indulgence through the rosary?" you ask. It's easy!

The Catholic Church has a book called the *Manual of Indulgences.* In this book, the Church gives us the "Norms" and "Grants" on how indulgences may be obtained. For your convenience, I have listed the pertinent norms and grants that deal with indulgences related to the rosary, focusing in particular on how often an indulgence may be obtained and what conditions must be met to gain it. Note: I have intentionally left out much of the lists because some aspects of the norms and grants are not related to the rosary.

NORMS

n. 3 — The faithful can obtain partial or plenary indulgences for themselves, or they can apply them to the dead [souls in purgatory] by way of suffrage. [No one gaining an indulgence may apply it to other living persons].

n. 17 — In order to be capable of gaining indulgences one must be baptized, not excommunicated, and in the state of grace at least at the completion of the prescribed works.

n. 18 — A plenary indulgence can be acquired only once in the course of a day; a partial indulgence can be acquired multiple times.

n. 20 — To gain a plenary indulgence, in addition to excluding all attachment to sin, even venial sin, it is necessary to perform the indulgenced work and fulfill the following three conditions: sacramental confession, Eucharistic Communion, and prayer for the intention of the Sovereign Pontiff [the Holy Father].

* The three conditions [in n. 20 above] may be fulfilled several days before or after the performance of the prescribed work; it is, however fitting that Communion be received and the prayer for the intention of the Holy Father be said on the same day the work is performed.

* The condition of praying for the intention of the Holy Father is fully satisfied by reciting one Our Father and one Hail Mary; nevertheless, one has the option of reciting any other prayer according to individual piety and devotion, if recited for this intention.

GRANTS

n. 17 — Prayers to the Blessed Virgin Mary

A plenary indulgence is granted to the faithful who:

- Devoutly recite the Marian rosary in a church or oratory, or in a family, a religious community, or an association of the faithful, and in general when several of the faithful gather for some honest purpose;

- Devoutly join in the recitation of the rosary while it is being recited by the Supreme Pontiff and broadcast live by radio or television. In other circumstances, the indulgence will be *partial*.

NB: According to the *Manual of Indulgences*, the plenary indulgence offered for praying the rosary is gained when only five decades of the rosary are recited. However, the five decades must be recited without interruption.[9]

In light of the above, is it now clear why the Church has constantly promoted the Family Rosary? It should be. By praying the Family Rosary in the home, each member of a family can gain a plenary indulgence on a daily basis, provided they live a life in close union with the Sacraments of the Church and pray for the Holy Father. It doesn't get any easier than this!

So many popes have placed such importance on the Family Rosary because it offers a great way to grow in virtue and gain a daily plenary indulgence. For example, look at the teachings of Blessed Pope Pius IX. Now, Pius IX was a great pope for a lot of reasons, including the fact that he defined the dogma of the Immaculate Conception in 1854. During the ceremony for the definition, he broke down and cried because he was aware of the great blessing that had been entrusted to him. Yet out of everything else he could have prioritized, do you know what his last message to the world focused on, delivered shortly before he died? It was about the Family Rosary and its indulgences. He said:

> Let the rosary, this simple, beautiful method of prayer, enriched with many indulgences, be habitually recited in the evening in every household. These are my last words to you: the memorial I leave behind me.[10]

The 15 Promises of Our Lady to Those Who Pray the Rosary

According to tradition, the rosary has been blessed by Our Lady with 15 promises of special graces.

Two of the greatest Marian saints of all time had this to say about these promises and the indulgences that go with the rosary:

> I promise you that if you practice this devotion [the rosary] and help to spread it you will learn more from the rosary than from any spiritual book. And what is more, you will have the happiness of being rewarded by Our Lady in accordance with the promises that she made to Saint Dominic, to Blessed Alan de la Roche and to all those who practice and encourage this devotion which is so dear to her. For the holy rosary teaches

people about the virtues of Jesus and Mary, and leads them to mental prayer and to imitate Our Lord and Savior Jesus Christ. It teaches them to approach the Sacraments often, to genuinely strive after Christian virtues and to do all kinds of good works, as well as interesting them in the many wonderful indulgences which can be gained through the rosary.[11]

St. Louis de Montfort

There is often mention of fifteen promises, by means of which the Most Blessed Virgin exhorts the faithful to recite the rosary. Those who received these promises were St. Dominic and Bl. Alan de la Roche.[12]

St. Maximilian Kolbe

The 15 Promises:

1) To all those who shall recite my rosary devoutly, I promise my special protection and very great graces.

2) Those who shall persevere in the recitation of my rosary shall receive signal graces.

3) The rosary shall be a very powerful armor against hell; it will destroy vice, deliver from sin, and dispel heresy.

4) The rosary will make virtue and good works flourish, and will obtain for souls the most abundant divine mercies; it will draw the hearts of men from the love of the world to the love of God, and will lift them to the desire of eternal things. How many souls shall sanctify themselves by this means!

5) Those who trust themselves to me through the rosary shall not perish.

6) Those who shall recite my rosary devoutly, meditating on its mysteries, shall not be overwhelmed by misfortune. The sinner shall be converted; the just shall grow in grace and become worthy of eternal life.

7) Those truly devoted to my rosary shall not die without the Sacraments of the Church.

8) Those who faithfully recite my rosary shall find during their life and at the hour of their death the light of God, the fullness of his graces, and shall share in the merits of the blessed.

9) I shall deliver very promptly from purgatory the souls devoted to my rosary.

10) The true children of my rosary shall enjoy great glory in heaven.

11) What you ask through my rosary, you shall obtain.

12) Those who propagate my rosary will be aided by me in all their necessities.

13) I have obtained from my Son that all the members of the Rosary Confraternity shall have as their intercessors, in life and in death, the entire celestial court.

14) Those who recite my rosary faithfully are all my beloved children, the brothers and sisters of Jesus Christ.

15) Devotion to my rosary is a great sign of predestination.[13]

WORDS OF WONDER

People are often quite unaware of how rich the rosary is in indulgences. This is because many priests, when preaching on the rosary, hardly ever mention indulgences and give rather a flowery and popular sermon which excites admiration but scarcely teaches anything.[14]

St. Louis de Montfort

Let all the children of Saint Dominic rise up for the fight and let them, like mighty warriors, be prepared to use in the battle the weapons with which their blessed Father, with so much foresight, armed them. This is what they have to do: Let them plant everywhere the rosary of the Blessed Virgin Mary; let them propagate and cultivate it with fervor; through their assiduous care may the nations be enrolled in these holy militias where the ensigns of the rosary shine; may the faithful learn to avail themselves of this weapon, to use it frequently; may they be instructed in the benefits, graces, and privileges of this devotion.[15]

Pope Leo XIII

Suffice it to know that this devotion [the rosary] has been approved by the Church, and that the Sovereign Pontiffs have enriched it with indulgences.[16]

St. Alphonsus Liguori

BONUS WONDER

PRAYING THE ROSARY MAKES REPARATION TO THE IMMACULATE HEART OF MARY

I would guess that most people who have read this book are familiar with the apparitions that took place in Fatima, Portugal, in 1917. On six different occasions from May 13 to October 13, the Mother of God appeared to three little children (Sts. Jacinta and Francisco Marto, and the Servant of God Lucia Dos Santos). Our Lady instructed the children about the importance of prayer (especially the rosary), penance, and making reparation to the Immaculate Heart of Mary. According to the visionaries, the rosary was the most important aspect of the Fatima apparitions; during the last apparition (October 13, 1917), Mary even identified herself as "The Lady of the Rosary."

And yet, did you know that Sr. Lucia Dos Santos continued to receive apparitions after 1917? Did you know that Jesus and Mary asked for a specific form of devotion known as the Five First Saturdays, a method of devotion that is intended to make reparation to the Immaculate Heart of Mary?

Here's what you need to know:

After the apparitions in Fatima, Portugal, which ended in 1917, Mary appeared again to Sr. Lucia on December 10, 1925, at the convent where she lived in Pontevedra, Spain. It was during this apparition that Our Lady spoke to Sr. Lucia about the Five First Saturdays of reparation. Mary explained their importance in the following words:

> See, my daughter, my heart, encircled by thorns with which ungrateful men pierce it at every moment by their blasphemies and ingratitude. Do you, at least, strive to console me. Tell them that I promise to assist at the hour of death with the graces necessary for salvation all those who, in order to make reparation to me, on the First Saturday of five successive months, go to Confession, receive Holy Communion, say five decades of the rosary, and keep me company for a quarter of an hour, meditating on the mysteries of the rosary.[1]

This means that, when we pray the rosary as part of the Five First Saturdays devotion, we console our spiritual mother and make reparation to her Immaculate Heart! What a wonder!

But there's more!

Like the 15 promises that Mary had revealed to St. Dominic and Bl. Alan de la Roche about the rosary, Mary promised to Sr. Lucia and to all those who make the Five First Saturdays devotion that she would assist them at the hour of their death with the graces necessary for salvation. This is an offer we can't refuse!

Now, you might wonder, "Why only five Saturdays? Why not seven, eight, 10, or 12 Saturdays?" Sister Lucia herself wondered about this. Jesus explained this to her on May 29–30, 1930, saying:

> Daughter, the motive is simple: There are five kinds of offenses and blasphemies spoken against the Immaculate Heart of Mary.
>
> > **First:** blasphemies against the Immaculate Conception
> >
> > **Second:** against her Virginity
> >
> > **Third:** against the Divine Maternity, refusing, at the same time, to receive her as the Mother of mankind
> >
> > **Fourth:** those who seek publicly to implant, in the hearts of children, indifference, disrespect, and even hate for this Immaculate Mother

Fifth: those who revile her directly in her sacred images.

Here, dear daughter, is the motive that led the Immaculate Heart of Mary to petition me to ask for this small act of reparation.[2]

In response to the request of Jesus and Mary, let's carry out this wonder of the rosary and make reparation to the Immaculate Heart of Mary, our spiritual mother. Here's all you have to do on the first Saturdays of five consecutive months with the intention of making reparation to the Immaculate Heart:

- Go to Confession
- Receive Holy Communion
- Pray five decades of the rosary
- Meditate for 15 minutes on the mysteries of the rosary. (This is in addition to praying five decades of the rosary.)

ADDENDUM

SAINT DOMINIC:
FOUNDER OF THE ROSARY

In *Wonder 1*, I present to the reader the long-standing tradition within the Catholic Church that St. Dominic is the founder of the rosary. This tradition is known as the "pious tradition." Unfortunately, over the last several centuries, some practitioners of the historical-critical method, revisionists of history, and modernists have attempted to refute the pious tradition. For those who would like to learn more about the veracity of this tradition, I highly recommend obtaining a copy of my book *Champions of the Rosary: The History and Heroes of a Spiritual Weapon*. In *Champions of the Rosary*, I present a thoroughly researched and well-documented defense of the pious tradition.

In addition to the wonder of the miraculous image of Our Lady of Las Lajas (see Wonder 1), I present below another wonder of the rosary: the apparitions of Our Lady in Cuapa, Nicaragua. These apparitions have received the approval of the local bishop, and offer us further insight into the true origins of the rosary.

The Marian Apparitions in Cuapa, Nicaragua

In May of 1980, Our Lady began appearing to a 49-year-old sacristan named Bernardo Martinez in rural Nicaragua. Bernardo was a simple man, quite poor, and not well educated. Though Mary would only appear to him several times, the messages she delivered were very powerful. The rosary is considered *the* primary theme of the Cuapa apparitions. She instructed him about the importance of the daily rosary, told him to make sure to pray it with devotion, and also showed him a vision of the origins of the rosary, about which he knew absolutely nothing. She also taught him the Five First Saturdays devotion and told him that she didn't want the people to only pray the rosary during the month of May (a common practice in that region). Rather, she wanted the rosary prayed every month and every day. She particularly stressed the importance of praying the rosary as a family. Bernardo was so transformed by these messages that he discerned a vocation to become a priest. After many years of study, he was ordained in 1995 at the age of 64. He faithfully served as a priest for five years before dying on October 30, 2000, at the age of 69.

During the first apparition of Mary, Bernardo was informed by Mary that she wanted people to pray the rosary every day. She also informed him that she was not pleased when the rosary was prayed mechanically or in a rushed manner, and recommended that Bernardo and others pray the rosary with the aid of biblical excerpts. Not knowing exactly what Mary meant, Bernardo confessed to Our Lady that he was unaware that the rosary was a biblical prayer and asked her to tell him where he could find the relevant biblical passages. In response, Mary directed him to look up certain passages from the Bible. During this first apparition, Mary also instructed Bernardo to renew the practice of the Five First Saturdays devotion. Bernardo admitted that in earlier years, the people in his area had performed this practice faithfully, but, over time, it had fallen into disuse.

During his second vision, on June 8, 1980, Bernardo was shown the history of the rosary. At one point during the vision, Mary instructed Bernardo to look up at the sky. When he looked up, he saw something like a movie playing before him. He witnessed a large procession of saints dressed in white singing joyfully and beautifully. At the head of the procession were the early Christians, catechumens, and martyrs. As he saw this scene, Mary asked Bernardo if he wanted to be a martyr. He was not sure what it meant to be a martyr, and so Mary explained to him that it meant dying for one's faith. After seeing the procession of martyrs, there followed a group of saints dressed in white and carrying luminous rosaries in their hands. The rosaries had extremely white beads and gave off light in a variety of different colors. What Bernardo saw next is given in translation below. These are his own words, taken from the account he gave at the request of the local bishop:

> One of them [the saints dressed in white in the procession] carried a very large open book. He would read, and after listening, they silently meditated. They appeared to be in prayer.

> After this period of prayer and silence, they then prayed the Our Father and ten Hail Marys. I prayed with them. When the rosary was finished, Our Lady said to me: "These

are the first ones to whom I gave the rosary. That is the way that I want all of you to pray the rosary." I answered the Lady that yes we would. Some persons have told me that this possibly has to do with the Dominicans. I do not know that religious Order, and to this date have never seen anyone from that Order.

Afterwards, I saw a third group, all of them dressed in brown robes. But these I recognized as being similar to the Franciscans. Always the same, with rosaries and praying.

As they were passing after having prayed, Our Lady again told me: "These received the rosary from the hands of the first ones." After this, a fourth group was arriving. It was a huge procession now, as we are dressed [in lay clothes]. It was such a big group that it would be impossible to count them. In the earlier ones, I saw many men and women; but now, it was like an army in size, and they carried rosaries in their hands. They were dressed normally in all colors.[1]

The above account is extremely important from an historical perspective. Though St. Dominic is not named, it is obvious he is the one at the beginning of the procession carrying the very large open book.

It is a subtle affirmation of the pious tradition. The vision also underscores that it was from the Dominicans that the Franciscans and all others received the rosary. All in all, Mary's vision to Bernardo offers an affirmation of the pious tradition exactly as it has been presented in the oral tradition of the Church and the writings of the popes and saints.

HOW TO PRAY
THE ROSARY

Praying the Rosary

1. Make the Sign of the Cross and say the "Apostles' Creed."

2. Say the "Our Father."

3. Say three "Hail Marys."

4. Say the "Glory be to the Father."

5. Announce the First Mystery; then say the "Our Father."

6. Say 10 "Hail Marys" while meditating on the Mystery.

7. Say the "Glory be to the Father." After each decade, say the following prayer requested by the Blessed

Virgin Mary at Fatima: "O my Jesus, forgive us our sins, save us from the fires of hell. Lead all souls to Heaven, especially those in most need of Thy Mercy."

8. Announce the Second Mystery: then say the "Our Father." Repeat 6 and 7 and continue with the Third, Fourth, and Fifth Mysteries in the same manner.

9. Say the "Hail, Holy Queen" and the concluding prayer on the medal after the five decades are completed.

As a general rule, depending on the liturgical season, the various Mysteries of the rosary are prayed on the following days of the week:

SUNDAY:	Glorious Mysteries
MONDAY:	Joyful Mysteries
TUESDAY:	Sorrowful Mysteries
WEDNESDAY:	Glorious Mysteries
THURSDAY:	Luminous Mysteries
FRIDAY:	Sorrowful Mysteries
SATURDAY:	Joyful Mysteries

Prayers of the Rosary

THE SIGN OF THE CROSS

In the name of the Father, and of the Son, and of the Holy Spirit. Amen.

THE APOSTLES' CREED

I believe in God, the Father almighty, Creator of heaven and earth, and in Jesus Christ, his only Son, our Lord, who was conceived by the Holy Spirit, born of the Virgin Mary, suffered under Pontius Pilate, was crucified, died, and was buried; he descended into hell; on the third day he rose again from the dead; he ascended into heaven, and is seated at the right hand of God the Father almighty; from there he will come to judge the living and the dead. I believe in the Holy Spirit, the holy catholic Church, the communion of saints, the forgiveness of sins, the resurrection of the body, and life everlasting. Amen.

The wording of the Apostles' Creed conforms with the Roman Missal.

OUR FATHER

Our Father, who art in heaven; hallowed be Thy name; Thy kingdom come; Thy will be done on earth as it is in heaven. Give us this day our daily bread; and forgive us our trespasses as we forgive those who trespass against us, and lead us not into temptation; but deliver us from evil. Amen.

HAIL MARY

Hail Mary, full of grace. The Lord is with thee. Blessed art thou among women, and blessed is the fruit of thy womb, Jesus. Holy Mary, Mother of God, pray for us sinners, now and at the hour of our death. Amen.

GLORY BE TO THE FATHER

Glory be to the Father, and to the Son, and to the Holy Spirit. As it was in the beginning, is now, and ever shall be, world without end. Amen.

FATIMA PRAYER

O my Jesus, forgive us our sins, save us from the fires of hell. Lead all souls to Heaven, especially those most in need of Thy mercy.

HAIL, HOLY QUEEN

Hail, Holy Queen, Mother of Mercy, our life, our sweetness, and our hope, to thee do we cry, poor banished children of Eve; to thee do we send up our sighs, mourning and weeping in this valley of tears; turn, then, most gracious Advocate, thine eyes of mercy towards us, and after this, our exile, show unto us the blessed fruit of thy womb, Jesus. O clement, O loving, O sweet Virgin Mary!

Pray for us, O holy Mother of God, that we may be made worthy of the promises of Christ.

CONCLUDING PRAYER

O God, whose only begotten Son, by His life, death, and resurrection, has purchased for us the rewards of eternal life, grant, we beseech Thee, that by meditating on these mysteries of the most holy Rosary of the Blessed Virgin Mary, we may imitate what they contain and obtain what they promise, through the same Christ our Lord. Amen.

Mysteries of the Rosary

JOYFUL MYSTERIES

FIRST JOYFUL MYSTERY
THE ANNUNCIATION

And when the angel had come to her, he said, "Hail, full of grace, the Lord is with you" (Lk 1:28).

One Our Father, 10 Hail Marys, One Glory Be, etc.

FRUIT OF THE MYSTERY: *HUMILITY*

SECOND JOYFUL MYSTERY
THE VISITATION

Elizabeth, filled with the holy Spirit, cried out in a loud voice and said, "Most blessed are you among women, and blessed is the fruit of your womb" (Lk 1:41-42).

One Our Father, 10 Hail Marys, One Glory Be, etc.

FRUIT OF THE MYSTERY: *LOVE OF NEIGHBOR*

THIRD JOYFUL MYSTERY
THE BIRTH OF JESUS

She gave birth to her firstborn Son. She wrapped Him in swaddling clothes and laid Him in a manger, because there was no room for them in the inn (Lk 2:7).

One Our Father, 10 Hail Marys, One Glory Be, etc.

FRUIT OF THE MYSTERY: *POVERTY IN SPIRIT*

FOURTH JOYFUL MYSTERY
THE PRESENTATION

When the days were completed for their purification according to the law of Moses, they took Him up to Jerusalem to present Him to the Lord, just as it is written in the law of the Lord, "Every male that opens the womb shall be consecrated to the Lord" (Lk 2:22-23).

One Our Father, 10 Hail Marys, One Glory Be, etc.

FRUIT OF THE MYSTERY: *OBEDIENCE*

FIFTH JOYFUL MYSTERY
FINDING THE CHILD JESUS IN THE TEMPLE

After three days they found Him in the temple, sitting in the midst of the teachers, listening to them and asking them questions (Lk 2:46).

One Our Father, 10 Hail Marys, One Glory Be, etc.

FRUIT OF THE MYSTERY: *JOY IN FINDING JESUS*

LUMINOUS MYSTERIES

FIRST LUMINOUS MYSTERY
BAPTISM OF JESUS

After Jesus was baptized, ... the heavens were opened [for Him], and he saw the Spirit of God descending like a dove [and] coming upon Him. And a voice came from the heavens, saying, "This is My beloved Son, with whom I am well pleased" (Mt 3:16-17).

One Our Father, 10 Hail Marys, One Glory Be, etc.

FRUIT OF THE MYSTERY: *OPENNESS TO THE HOLY SPIRIT*

SECOND LUMINOUS MYSTERY
WEDDING AT CANA

His mother said to the servers, "Do whatever He tells you." ... Jesus told them, "Fill the jars with water." So they filled them to the brim (Jn 2:5-7).

One Our Father, 10 Hail Marys, One Glory Be, etc.

FRUIT OF THE MYSTERY: *TO JESUS THROUGH MARY*

THIRD LUMINOUS MYSTERY
PROCLAIMING THE KINGDOM

"As you go, make this proclamation: 'The kingdom of heaven is at hand.' Cure the sick, raise the dead, cleanse lepers, drive out demons. Without cost you have received; without cost you are to give" (Mt 10:7-8).

One Our Father, 10 Hail Marys, One Glory Be, etc.

FRUIT OF THE MYSTERY: *REPENTANCE AND TRUST IN GOD*

FOURTH LUMINOUS MYSTERY
TRANSFIGURATION

While He was praying His face changed in appearance and His clothing became dazzling white. Then from the cloud came a voice that said, "This is My chosen Son; listen to Him" (Lk 9:29, 35).

One Our Father, 10 Hail Marys, One Glory Be, etc.

FRUIT OF THE MYSTERY: *DESIRE FOR HOLINESS*

FIFTH LUMINOUS MYSTERY
INSTITUTION OF THE EUCHARIST

Then He took the bread, said the blessing, broke it, and gave it to them, saying, "This is My body, which will be given for you ..." And likewise the cup after they had eaten, saying, "This cup is the new covenant in My blood" (Lk 22:19-20).

One Our Father, 10 Hail Marys, One Glory Be, etc.

FRUIT OF THE MYSTERY: *ADORATION*

SORROWFUL MYSTERIES

FIRST SORROWFUL MYSTERY
THE AGONY IN THE GARDEN

He was in such agony and He prayed so fervently that His sweat became like drops of blood falling on the ground. When He rose from prayer and returned to His disciples, He found them sleeping from grief (Lk 22:44-45).

One Our Father, 10 Hail Marys, One Glory Be, etc.

FRUIT OF THE MYSTERY: *SORROW FOR SIN*

SECOND SORROWFUL MYSTERY
THE SCOURGING AT THE PILLAR

Then Pilate took Jesus and had Him scourged (Jn 19:1).

One Our Father, 10 Hail Marys, One Glory Be, etc.

FRUIT OF THE MYSTERY: *PURITY*

THIRD SORROWFUL MYSTERY
CROWNING WITH THORNS

They stripped off His clothes and threw a scarlet military cloak about Him. Weaving a crown out of thorns, they placed it on His head, and a reed in His right hand (Mt 27:28-29).

One Our Father, 10 Hail Marys, One Glory Be, etc.

FRUIT OF THE MYSTERY: *COURAGE*

FOURTH SORROWFUL MYSTERY
CARRYING OF THE CROSS

And carrying the cross Himself, He went out to what is called the Place of the Skull, in Hebrew, Golgotha (Jn 19:17).

One Our Father, 10 Hail Marys, One Glory Be, etc.

FRUIT OF THE MYSTERY: *PATIENCE*

FIFTH SORROWFUL MYSTERY
THE CRUCIFIXION

Jesus cried out in a loud voice, "Father, into Your hands I commend My spirit"; and when He had said this He breathed His last (Lk 23:46).

One Our Father, 10 Hail Marys, One Glory Be, etc.

FRUIT OF THE MYSTERY: *PERSEVERANCE*

GLORIOUS MYSTERIES

FIRST GLORIOUS MYSTERY
THE RESURRECTION

"Do not be amazed! You seek Jesus of Nazareth, the crucified. He has been raised; He is not here. Behold the place where they laid Him" (Mk16:6).

One Our Father, 10 Hail Marys, One Glory Be, etc.

FRUIT OF THE MYSTERY: *FAITH*

SECOND GLORIOUS MYSTERY
THE ASCENSION

So then the Lord Jesus, after He spoke to them, was taken up into heaven and took His seat at the right hand of God (Mk 16:19).

One Our Father, 10 Hail Marys, One Glory Be, etc.

FRUIT OF THE MYSTERY: *HOPE*

THIRD GLORIOUS MYSTERY
DESCENT OF THE HOLY SPIRIT

And they were all filled with the Holy Spirit and began to speak in different tongues, as the Spirit enabled them to proclaim (Acts 2:4).

One Our Father, 10 Hail Marys, One Glory Be, etc.

FRUIT OF THE MYSTERY: *LOVE OF GOD*

FOURTH GLORIOUS MYSTERY
THE ASSUMPTION

"You are the glory of Jerusalem! ... You are the great boast of our nation! ... You have done good things for Israel, and God is pleased with them. May the Almighty Lord bless you forever!" (Jud 15:9-10).

One Our Father, 10 Hail Marys, One Glory Be, etc.

FRUIT OF THE MYSTERY: *GRACE OF A HAPPY DEATH*

FIFTH GLORIOUS MYSTERY
THE CORONATION

A great sign appeared in the sky, a woman clothed with the sun, with the moon under her feet, and on her head a crown of twelve stars (Rev 12:1).

One Our Father, 10 Hail Marys, One Glory Be, etc.

FRUIT OF THE MYSTERY: *TRUST IN MARY'S INTERCESSION*

REFERENCES

* Initial quotes at the beginning of the book:

– St. Louis de Montfort, *The Secret of the Rosary,* trans. Mary Barbour, TOP (Bay Shore, NY: Montfort Publications, 1988), 29.

FOREWORD

(1) St. Louis de Montfort, *The Secret of the Rosary.* trans. Mary Barbour, TOP (Bay Shore, New York: Montfort Publications, 1988), 33.

WONDER 1

(1) Pope Leo XIII, *Parta Humano Generi,* Apostolic Letter (September 8, 1901), in *The Rosary of Our Lady: Translations of the Encyclical and Apostolic Letters of Pope Leo XIII,* ed. William Raymond Lawler, OP (Paterson, NJ: St. Anthony Guild Press, 1944), 195-196.

(2) "*Our Lady's words to St. Dominic,*" as quoted in Augusta Theodosia Drane, OP, *The History of St. Dominic: Founder of the Friars Preachers* (London: Longmans, Green, and Co., 1891), 122.

(3) "*Our Lady's words to St. Dominic,*" as quoted in St. Louis de Montfort, *The Secret of the Rosary.* Trans. Mary Barbour, TOP (Bay Shore, NY: Montfort Publications, 1988), 18.

(4) St. Louis de Montfort, *The Secret of the Rosary,* trans. Mary Barbour, TOP (Bay Shore, NY: Montfort Publications, 1988), 27.

(5) Sister Lúcia Dos Santos, as quoted in Fr. Robert Fox, *The Intimate Life of Sister Lucia* (USA: Fatima Family Apostolate, 2001), 315.

(6) Ven. Pope Pius XII, *Ingruentium Malorum,* Encyclical (September 15, 1951), 8.

(7) Blessed James Alberione, *Mary, Mother and Model: Feasts of Mary,* trans. Hilda Calabro, MA (Boston, MA: Daughters of St. Paul, 1958), 200.

(8) St. Maximilian Kolbe, as quoted in Hilda Elfleda Brown, *She Shall Crush Thy Head: Selected Writings of St. Maximilian Kolbe* (Phoenix, AZ: Leonine Publishers, 2015), 40.

WONDER 2

(1) Blessed Pope Pius IX, as quoted in *The Official Handbook of the Legion of Mary* (Dublin: Concilium Legionis Mariae, 2005), 146.

(2) St. Albert the Great, as quoted in Beato Alano della Rupe, *Lo Splendore e il Valore del Santissimo Rosario (incunabolo del 1498): Libro II.* Translated from the Latin into Italian by Don Roberto Paola and Gaspare Paola. (Rome, Italy: Centro Studia Rosariana, 2017), 87. The English translation of the quote was graciously provided by Deacon Eduardo Fortini. Used with permission.

(3) St. Louis de Montfort, *The Secret of the Rosary.* trans. Mary Barbour, TOP (Bay Shore, NY: Montfort Publications, 1988), 46.

(4) Blessed James Alberione, *Mary, Mother and Model: Feasts of Mary,* trans. Hilda Calabro, MA (Boston, MA: Daughters of St. Paul, 1958), 201.

(5) Servant of God Joseph Kentenich, *Mary, Our Mother and Educator: An Applied Mariology,* trans. Jonathan Niehaus (Waukesha, WI: Schoenstatt Sisters, 1987), 11.

(6) Servant of God Dolindo Ruotolo, *Meditations on the Holy Rosary of Mary,* trans. Giovanna Invitti Ellis (Napoli, Italy, 2006), 36.

(7) Pope Benedict XVI, *Homily: Pastoral Visit to the Pontifical Shrine of Our Lady of the Rosary of Pompeii.* (October 19, 2008).

(8) Blessed Pope Pius IX, as quoted in Wilfrid Lescher, OP, *St. Dominic and the Rosary* (London: R. & T. Washbourne, 1902), 8-9.

(9) St. Josemaría Escrivá, *Holy Rosary* (New York, NY: Scepter Press, 2003), 9.

(10) Ven. Patrick Peyton, as quoted in *Rosary* [Revised edition of the special rosary issue of *The Immaculate* magazine, 1970], 40. Originally published in October 1965 (Vol. 16. No. 5).

WONDER 3

(1) St. Louis de Montfort, *The Secret of the Rosary,* trans. Mary Barbour, TOP (Bay Shore, NY: Montfort Publications, 1988), 93.

(2) St. Louis de Montfort, *The Secret of the Rosary,* trans. Mary Barbour, TOP (Bay Shore, NY: Montfort Publications, 1988), 30.

(3) St. Bonaventure, as quoted in St. Alphonsus Ligouri, *The Glories of Mary* (Rockford, IL: TAN, 1977), 122-123.

(4) St. Ignatius of Antioch, "Letter to the Ephesians," in *Early Christian Fathers,* Cyril C. Richardson, ed. (New York: MacMillan Company, 1970), 113.

(5) St. Pio of Pietrelcina, as quoted by Most Rev. Paola Carta (Bishop Emeritus of Foggia) in *From the Voice of Padre Pio* (July, 1997). Friary of Our Lady of Grace, San Giovanni Rotondo, Italy.

(6) Sister Lúcia Dos Santos, as quoted in Fr. Robert Fox, *The Intimate Life of Sister Lucia* (USA: Fatima Family Apostolate, 2001), 316.

(7) St. Anthony Mary Claret, as quoted in Fr. Juan Echevarria, *The Miracles of St. Anthony Mary Claret.* trans. Sr. Mary Gonzaga (Charlotte, NC: TAN Books, 1992), 61.

(8) St. Louis de Montfort, *The Secret of the Rosary,* trans. Mary Barbour, TOP (Bay Shore, NY: Montfort Publications, 1988), 98.

(9) Pope Leo XIII, *Parta Humano Generi*, Apostolic Letter (September 8, 1901), in *The Rosary of Our Lady: Translations of the Encyclical and Apostolic Letters of Pope Leo XIII*, ed. William Raymond Lawler, OP (Paterson, NJ: St. Anthony Guild Press, 1944), 195-196.

WONDER 4

(1) St. Anthony Mary Claret, *El Colegial Ó Seminarista Teórica y Prácticamente Instruido: Tome I* (Barcelona, Spain: Librería Religiosa, 1861), 276. Trans. Miss Ileana E. Salazar, MA.

(2) Blessed William Joseph Chaminade, *The Chaminade Legacy: Volume 2: Notes for Conferences and Sermons.* Trans. Joseph Stefanelli, SM (Dayton, Ohio: North American Center for Marianist Studies, 2008), 342.

(3) St. Anthony Mary Claret, *El Colegial Ó Seminarista Teórica y Prácticamente Instruido: Tome I* (Barcelona, Spain: Librería Religiosa, 1861), 276. Trans. Miss Ileana E. Salazar, MA.

(4) St. Maximilian Kolbe, "1021 — Arcybractwo Rózanca Sw"[Grodno 1922-1925] in *Pisma Sw Maksymiliana Kolbego* (Niepokalanów, Poland), trans. Fr. Thaddaeus Lancton, MIC, from the original Polish. In the Italian *Scritti di Massimiliano Kolbe* (Roma, 1997), it is found in section 1257 with a different, and inaccurate, translation.

(5) St. Louis de Montfort, *The Secret of the Rosary,* trans. Mary Barbour, TOP (Bay Shore, NY: Montfort Publications, 1988), 26.

(6) St. John Paul II, *Rosarium Virginis Mariae,* 26.

(7) Ven. Fulton J. Sheen, *The World's First Love: Mary, Mother of God* (San Francisco, CA: Ignatius Press, 1996), 208.

(8) Ven. Fulton J. Sheen, *The World's First Love: Mary, Mother of God* (San Francisco, CA: Ignatius Press, 1996), 207-208.

(9) St. Louis de Montfort, *The Secret of the Rosary,* trans. Mary Barbour, TOP (Bay Shore, NY: Montfort Publications, 1988), 26.

(10) St. Pope Paul VI, as quoted in *Rosary* (Revised edition of the special rosary issue of *The Immaculate* magazine, 1970), 10. Originally published in October 1965 (Vol.16. No.5).

(11) Ven. Pope Pius XII, *Letter to the Most Rev. Master General, Michael Browne, OP, concerning the Marian rosary* (July 11, 1957).

WONDER 5

(1) Ven. Fulton J. Sheen, *The World's First Love: Mary, Mother of God* (San Francisco, CA: Ignatius Press, 1996), 215.

(2) Sister Lúcia Dos Santos, as quoted in Fr. Robert Fox, *The Intimate Life of Sister Lucia* (USA: Fatima Family Apostolate, 2001), 316.

(3) St. Louis de Montfort, *The Secret of the Rosary*, trans. Mary Barbour, TOP (Bay Shore, NY: Montfort Publications, 1988), 78.

(4) Fr. Marie Étienne Vayssière, OP, as quoted in Gabriel Harty, OP, *Heaven Sent: My Life Through the Rosary* (Dublin, Ireland: Veritas, 2012), 105.

(5) Pope Pius XI, as quoted in Msgr. Joseph A. Cirrincione and Thomas A. Nelson, *The Rosary and the Crisis of Faith* (Charlotte, NC: TAN Books, 1986), 33.

(6) Ven. Patrick Peyton, *Marian Year: 1987-1988* (Albany, NY: The Family Rosary Inc., 1987), 75.

(7) John ab Eckersdorff, as quoted in Daniel Conway, "The Story of a Scottish Martyr," in *The Month and Catholic Review*, vol. 32, no. 13 (March 1878), 356-357.

(8) Blessed James Alberione, *Mary, Mother and Model: Feasts of Mary*, trans. Hilda Calabro, MA (Boston, MA: Daughters of St. Paul, 1958), 201.

(9) Pope Leo XIII, *Magnae Dei Matris*, Encyclical (September 8, 1892), 7.

(10) St. Louis de Montfort, *The Secret of the Rosary*, trans. Mary Barbour, TOP (Bay Shore, NY: Montfort Publications, 1988), 81.

WONDER 6

(1) St. Pope Paul VI, *Mense Maio,* Encyclical (April 29, 1965), 14.

(2) Ven. Pope Pius XII, *Mediator Dei,* Encyclical (November 20, 1947), 173-174.

(3) St. Pope John XXIII, as quoted in Andrew J. Gerakas, *The Rosary and Devotion to Mary* (Boston, MA: St. Paul Books & Media, 1992), 23.

(4) Ven. Patrick Peyton, in "Mary, the Pope, and the American Apostle of the Family Rosary," by Fr. Willy Raymond, CSC, in *Behold Your Mother: Priests Speak about Mary,* ed. Stephen J. Rossetti (Notre Dame, IN: Ave Maria Press, 2007), 53.

(5) St. John Paul II, *Angelus message* (October 1, 1995)

(6) St. John Paul II, *Rosarium Virginis Mariae,* 41.

(7) Pope Pius XI, *Ingravescentibus Malis,* Encyclical (September 29, 1937), 29.

(8) St. Pope Paul VI, *Marialis Cultus,* 52.

(9) St. John Paul II, *Rosarium Virginis Mariae,* 41.

WONDER 7

(1) Servant of God Frank Duff, *Virgo Praedicanda* (Dublin: Mount Salus Press, 1986), 98.

(2) St. John Paul II, *Homily* (May 4, 1997).

(3) Pope Benedict XVI, *Papal Address* (June 11, 2011).

(4) St. John Paul II, *Rosarium Virginis Mariae,* Apostolic Letter (October 16, 2002), 8.

(5) St. Francis de Sales, as quoted in Robert Feeney, *The Rosary: "The Little Summa,"* fourth edition (USA: Aquinas Press, 2003), 82.

(6) Pope Pius XI, *Iniquis Afflictisque* (*On the Persecution of the Church in Mexico.*) November 18, 1926. Encyclical Letter. Paragraph 27.

(7) St. Anthony Mary Claret, *El Colegial Ó Seminarista Teórica y Prácticamente Instruido: Tome I* (Barcelona, Spain: Librería Religiosa, 1861), 276. Trans. Miss Ileana E. Salazar, MA.

(8) St. Thérèse of Lisieux, as quoted in Romanus Cessario, OP, *Perpetual Angelus: As the Saints Pray the Rosary* (Staten Island, NY: Alba House, 1995), 136.

(9) St. Louis de Montfort, *The Secret of the Rosary,* trans. Mary Barbour, TOP (Bay Shore, NY: Montfort Publications, 1988), 103, 105-106.

(10) St. Teresa of Calcutta, *Heart of Joy* (Ann Arbor, MI: Servant Books, 1987), 19.

(11) St. Pope John XXIII, "*Radio Message for the Coronation of Our Lady of the Rosary of La Coruña, Spain*" (September 11, 1960). Trans. Miss Ileana E. Salazar, MA.

(12) Ven. Fulton J. Sheen, *The World's First Love: Mary, Mother of God* (San Francisco, CA: Ignatius Press, 1996), 213.

(13) St. John Paul II, *Rosarium Virginis Mariae,* 43.

WONDER 8

(1) Servant of God Joseph Kentenich, *Talk by Fr. Joseph Kentenich in the Church at Ennabeuren, Germany* (May 3, 1945). Courtesy of Schoenstatt Sisters, Waukesha, WI.

(2) St. Anthony Mary Claret, *El Colegial Ó Seminarista Teórica y Prácticamente Instruido: Tome I* (Barcelona, Spain: Librería Religiosa, 1861), 277. Trans. Miss Ileana E. Salazar, MA.

(3) Servant of God Frank Duff, *Virgo Praedicanda* (Dublin: Mount Salus Press, 1986), 98.

(4) Servant of God Joseph Kentenich, *Mary, Our Mother and Educator: An Applied Mariology,* trans. Jonathan Niehaus (Waukesha, WI: Schoenstatt Sisters, 1987), 11.

(5) Servant of God Lúcia Dos Santos, as quoted in Rory Michael Fox, *Saints, Popes and Blesseds Speak on the Rosary* [E-reader version], 2012.

(6) Servant of God Joseph Kentenich, *Mary, Our Mother and Educator: An Applied Mariology*, trans. Jonathan Niehaus (Waukesha, WI: Schoenstatt Sisters, 1987), 11.

(7) Blessed James Alberione, *Lord, Teach Us to Pray* (Boston, MA: Daughters of St. Paul, 1982), 226.

(8) Ven. Fulton J. Sheen, *The World's First Love: Mary, Mother of God* (San Francisco, CA: Ignatius Press, 1996), 211.

WONDER 9

(1) Pope Leo XIII, as quoted in Rev. J.A. Rooney, OP, "Rosary Sunday and Month: The Dominican Portiuncula," *The Rosary Magazine* (October, 1892), 453.

(2) Bishop Oliver Dashe Doeme, as quoted in Alan Holdren, "After vision of Christ, Nigerian bishop says rosary will bring down Boko Haram," *Catholic News Agency (CNA)*, April 21, 2015. Online edition.

(3) Servant of God Joseph Kentenich, as quoted in Fr. Jonathan Neihaus, *New Vision and Life: The Founding of Schoenstatt (1912-1919)* (Waukesha, WI: Schoenstatt Fathers, 2004), 35.

(4) Miguel Cervantes, as quoted in Rev. J.A. Rooney, OP, "Rosary Sunday and Month: The Dominican Portiuncula," *The Rosary Magazine* (October, 1892), 449-450.

(5) Ven. Fulton J. Sheen, *The World's First Love: Mary, Mother of God* (San Francisco, CA: Ignatius Press, 1996), 202.

(6) King Jan Sobieski, as quoted in Robert Debs Heinl, *Dictionary of Military and Naval Quotations* (Annapolis, MD: United States Naval Institute, 1966), 65.

(7) Pope Benedict XV, *Fausto Appetente Die*, Encyclical (June 29, 1921), 11.

(8) Ven. Fulton J. Sheen, *The World's First Love: Mary, Mother of God* (San Francisco, CA: Ignatius Press, 1996), 204.

(9) St. John Paul II, *Angelus message* (September 30, 2001).

WONDER 10

(1) Blessed James Alberione, *Mary, Mother and Model: Feasts of Mary,* trans. Hilda Calabro, MA (Boston, MA: Daughters of St. Paul, 1958), 201.

(2) *Catechism of the Catholic Church.* 2nd Edition (Citta del Vaticano: Libreria Editrice Vaticana, 1997), par. 1471.

(3) St. Louis de Montfort, *The Secret of the Rosary,* trans. Mary Barbour, TOP (Bay Shore, NY: Montfort Publications, 1988), 79.

(4) St. Alphonsus Liguori, as quoted in Susan Tassone, *Day By Day for the Holy Souls in Purgatory: 365 Reflections* (Huntington, IN: Our Sunday Visitor, Inc., 2014), 298.

(5) St. Louis de Montfort, *The Secret of the Rosary,* trans. Mary Barbour, TOP (Bay Shore, NY: Montfort Publications, 1988), 78-79.

(6) Blessed James Alberione, *Lest We Forget* (Boston, MA: Daughters of St. Paul, 1967), 96.

(7) St. Alphonsus Liguori, as quoted in Catherine Moran, *Praying the Rosary with the Saints* [E-reader version], 2013.

(8) St. Anthony Mary Claret, *El Colegial Ó Seminarista Teórica y Prácticamente Instruido: Tome I* (Barcelona, Spain: Librería Religiosa, 1861), 277. Trans. Miss Ileana E. Salazar, MA.

(9) *Manual of Indulgences: Norms and Grants.* United States Catholic Conference of Bishops Publishing (December 1, 2006).

(10) Blessed Pope Pius IX, as quoted in *Rosary* (Revised edition of the special rosary issue of *The Immaculate* magazine, 1970), 40. Originally published in vol. 16. no. 5 (October 1965).

(11) St. Louis de Montfort, *The Secret of the Rosary.* trans. Mary Barbour, TOP (Bay Shore, NY: Montfort Publications, 1988), 85.

(12) St. Maximilian Kolbe, *Scritti di Massimiliano Kolbe* (Roma, 1997), section 1021 [Grodno 1922-1925; The Archconfraternity of the Holy Rosary].

(13) Ven. Patrick Peyton, *The Ear of God* (Garden City, NJ: Doubleday & Company, Inc., 1951), 114-115.

(14) St. Louis de Montfort, *The Secret of the Rosary,* trans. Mary Barbour, TOP (Bay Shore, NY: Montfort Publications, 1988), 86.

(15) Pope Leo XIII, *Letter to the Master General of the Order of Preachers* (September 15, 1883).

(16) St. Alphonsus Liguori, *Hail Holy Queen: An Explanation of the Salve Regina.* (Charlotte, NC: TAN Books, 1995), 226.

BONUS WONDER

(1) See Fr. Donald Calloway, MIC, *Five First Saturdays in Reparation to the Immaculate Heart of Mary.* (Stockbridge, Massachusetts: Marian Press, 2017).

(2) Ibid.

ADDENDUM

(1) Bernardo Martinez, as quoted in *Apparitions of Our Blessed Mother at Cuapa, Nicaragua: A Report of the Events in Cuapa* (Washington, NJ: The World Apostolate of Fatima, 1982), 11.

About the Author

Father Donald Calloway, MIC, a convert to Catholicism, is a member of the Congregation of Marian Fathers of the Immaculate Conception. Before his conversion, he was a high school dropout who had been kicked out of a foreign country, institutionalized twice, and thrown in jail multiple times. After his radical conversion, he earned a BA in philosophy and theology from the Franciscan University of Steubenville, Ohio, MDiv and STB degrees from the Dominican House of Studies in Washington, D.C., and an STL in Mariology from the International Marian Research Institute in Dayton, Ohio.

In addition to *10 Wonders of the Rosary*, he has also written *26 Champions of the Rosary* (Marian Press, 2017), *How to Pray the Rosary* (Marian Press, 2017), the best-selling books *Champions of the Rosary: The History and Heroes of a Spiritual Weapon* (Marian Press, 2016); *Under the Mantle: Marian Thoughts from a 21st Century Priest* (Marian Press, 2013); and *No Turning Back: A Witness to Mercy* (Marian Press, 2010), a bestseller that recounts his dramatic conversion story. He also is the author of the book *Purest of All Lilies: The Virgin Mary in the Spirituality of St. Faustina* (Marian Press, 2008). He introduced and arranged *Marian Gems: Daily Wisdom on Our Lady* (Marian Press, 2014); *Rosary Gems: Daily Wisdom on the Holy Rosary* (Marian Press, 2015); and *St. Joseph Gems: Daily Wisdom on Our Spiritual Father* (Marian Press, 2018). Further, he has written many academic articles and is the editor of a number of books, including: *The Immaculate Conception in the Life of the Church* (Marian Press, 2004) and *The Virgin Mary and Theology of the Body* (Marian Press, 2005).

Father Calloway is the Vicar Provincial and Vocation Director for the Mother of Mercy Province.

To learn more about Marian
vocations, visit
marian.org/vocations
or visit
Fr. Calloway's website,
www.fathercalloway.com.

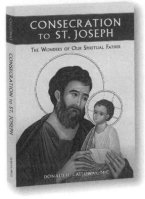

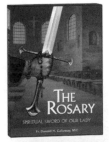

Marian Inspiration from Fr. Calloway

Champions of the Rosary
The History and Heroes of a Spiritual Weapon

Champions of the Rosary, by best-selling author Fr. Donald Calloway, MIC, tells the powerful story of the history of the Rosary and the champions of this devotion. The Rosary is a spiritual sword with the power to conquer sin, defeat evil, and bring about peace. Read this book to deepen your understanding of and love for praying the Rosary. Endorsed by 30 bishops from around the world! Paperback, 428 pages. Y79-CRBK [e]

How to Pray the Rosary
booklet

A Rosary a day keeps the devil away! In this handy little guide, best-selling author Fr. Donald Calloway, MIC, teaches you how to pray the Rosary well and why it matters. Our Lady needs Rosary champions to help bring peace into the world. Will you answer her call to prayer? Paperback, 72 pages. Y79-HPR [e]

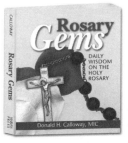

Rosary Gems
Daily Wisdom on the Holy Rosary

Inspired by his own love for the Rosary and the saints, Fr. Donald Calloway, MIC, has gathered and arranged into one book one of the largest collections of quotes on the Rosary to ever appear in print. The quotes have been selected from the writings of popes, saints, blesseds, and the many venerables of the Church. This is the perfect book to help you rediscover the power and wisdom of the holy Rosary! Paperback, 245 pages. Y79-RGEM

Call 1-800-462-7426 or visit www.fathercalloway.com